CADOGAN
guides

:e

Cadogan Books plc
27–29 Berwick Street
London W1V 3RF, UK

Distributed in the USA by
The Globe Pequot Press
6 Business Park Road, PO Box 833, Old Saybrook,
Connecticut 06475–0833

Copyright © Philippe Barbour, Dana Facaros,
Michael Pauls 1997
Illustrations © Charles Shearer 1997
Book, cover and map design by Animage
Cover photography and illustration
by Horacio Monteverde
Maps © Cadogan Guides, drawn by Animage
and Map Creation Ltd

Series editor: Rachel Fielding
Editing: Dominique Shead
Cookery editor: Michelle Clark

Production: Book Production Services
Printed and bound in the UK
by Redwood Books Ltd , Trowbridge

ISBN 1–86011–065–7
A catalogue record for this book is available
from the British Library

About the Author

Philippe Barbour is the author of the *Cadogan Guide to the Loire* and *Lazy Days Out in the Loire*, as well as co-author of *Wine Buyer's Guide: Saint Emilion*. He recently edited the *European Union Handbook* (published by Fitzroy Dearborn) and is now preparing the *Cadogan Guide to Brittany*.

Dana Facaros and Michael Pauls have written over 20 books for Cadogan, including the *Cadogan Guide to the South of France* and the *Cadogan Guide to Provence*. They live in a leaky old farmhouse in southwest France with their two children and assorted animals.

Acknowledgements

Enormous thanks from Philippe Barbour to his *ratatouille* of a research team, notably Kate Berney and David Lamb, and most especially to his parents, who helped in good part to sponsor the research for this guide. He would also like to thank the Provence tourist authorities for their assistance, in particular: Sylvie Keulian and Corinne Moulet of the CRT Provence Alpes Côte d'Azur; Bernard Chouial of the CDT Alpes-de-Haute-Provence; Danièle Damiani of the CDT Vaucluse; Sandrine Matard of the CDT Bouches-du-Rhône; and Sylvie Schmitt of the CDT Var. Many thanks too to the Maison de la France in London.

Please help us keep this guide up to date

Every effort has been made to ensure the accuracy of the information in this book at the time of going to press. However, standards in restaurants and practical details such as opening times and, in particular, prices are liable to change. We would be delighted to receive any comments concerning existing entries or indeed any sugestions for inclusion in future editions or companion volumes. Significant contributions will be acknowledged in the next edition, and authors of the best letters will receive a copy of the Cadogan Guide of their choice.

Contents

Introduction

Frédéric Mistral, spirited champion of the revival of Provençal culture in the 19th century, called his nationalist Provençal magazine *Aïoli*, the name of a Provençal mayonnaise! Importantly, *aïoli*, the mayonnaise, includes a couple of the basics of Provençal cuisine in its preparation—the egg yolks are mixed with garlic and olive oil.

Pernes-les-Fontaines

In virtually every restaurant you travel to in this book you'll be served either a bowl of olives with your *apéritif* or *tapenade*, the maturely salty purée of olives, olive oil and capers (some throw in the odd anchovy). The olive welcome may be similar across Provence, but in this guide we take you on twenty days out to explore many varied and splendid corners of four of the most blissful *départements* in France: the Vaucluse, the Bouches-du-Rhône, the Alpes-de-Haute-Provence, and the Var. And each restaurant recommended for each day has its own distinct character and cooking.

The twenty days of touring and tasting start in northern Vaucluse and move down the Rhône valley, Provence's burly western frontier, into the Bouches-du-Rhône and the salty Camargue. It's then metropolitan Provence to the east, with restaurants in Salon-de-Provence (the town where Nostradamus wrote not only his overanalyzed *Centuries* but also his healthy jam recipes), Marseille (Pagnol's metropolis) and Aix-en-Provence (the city that spurned Cézanne).

We pass through the Lubéron, Peter Mayle as well as Albert Camus country, on to the Durance valley, its countryside and deeper rural ways sung by Jean Giono. The diverse corners of the Alpes-de-Haute-Provence *département* are much less well known than the Vaucluse, particularly around the Mont Ventoux's eastern twin, the equally bald and spectacular Montagne de Lure. Lavender, almonds and truffles thrive on the barren plateau of Valensole close to Europe's grandest canyon and the Gorges du Verdon. We then take a quick look at the Provençal Alps at cheerful St-André-les-Alpes before finishing in the villages and vineyards of the northern Var.

Returning to the theme of Provençal food, though, the role of the ubiquitous olive in cooking here is hard to exaggerate. The history books say that the Greeks brought over the first trees around 600 BC; today's groves beautify several corners of Provence.

Many of the stock Provençal herbs grow wild on the region's hillsides—and you'll find bags of dried *herbes de Provence* on sale everywhere. Rosemary and thyme proliferate in particular. Another extremely popular herb is basil, which goes into *pistou*, mixed with garlic and parmesan. Lavender, an essential ingredient of the Provençal landscape, can also pop up on the menu, with lavender honey, lavender sorbet or even little lavender stems hidden in a sauce or a pudding.

The fruit and vegetables of Provence are almost as legendary as its lavender, making for the brightest of markets. A classic Provençal dish is *ratatouille*. The stock ingredients are splendid aubergines (eggplants), courgettes (zucchini), tomatoes, peppers, onions and garlic. The vegetables should be cooked separately first to keep the individual flavours before you bring them all together in olive oil. *Pomme d'amour* (love apple) is the rather sickly romantic name given to tomatoes in the region. They add their rich taste to innumerable dishes, although they were only introduced relatively recently in historical terms. Stuffed vegetables appear frequently on menus too. You may even get the chance to taste stuffed courgette flowers. Autumn brings the wonders of wild mushrooms, as well as pumpkins and squashes, which double in savoury and sweet recipes. Menus clearly vary according to the season.

The Mediterranean is never that far away, so Provençal fish should be good. *Rascasse*, *St-Pierre*, *lotte* and *vive* form the backbone of Marseille's famous seafood dish, *bouillabaisse*. Eels, leeks and saffron should also all put in an appearance, as may certain shellfish. You'll find many bastardized versions of *bouillabaisse* served up in Provence. It should come with a *rouille*, another stock Provençal sauce, containing garlic, egg yolks, saffron, chilli or cayenne pepper, and some fish stock. *Bourride* is the next best-known Provençal fish soup, made without any shellfish, often served with an *aïoli*. *Le grand aïoli*, by the way, was a traditional Catholic Friday dish, the garlic mayonnaise accompanying salt cod, a variety of vegetables, and possibly snails. Salt cod crops up time and again in Provence, in no better form than in the fantastic *brandade de morue*, garlic, olive oil and cream mixed in with it. Other popular and tasty fish include tuna and *rouget*, red mullet, while grey mullet eggs are used to make the unusual *poutargue* paste. *Loup* when it appears on a Provençal menu doesn't usually refer to wolf but to *loup de mer*, sea bass.

Distinctive meat, apart from lamb and Camargue bull, is less a feature of Provençal cooking. There are the *daubes*, slowly cooked stews, with herbs aplenty and often olives thrown in. One of the Provençal cook's prize possessions is his or her *daube* pan, which is never washed, but wiped clean and baked to form a crust that flavours the subsequent stews. *Estouffades* are another type of Provençal stew, also using plenty of Provençal wine. The wild or reared animals of the *garrigues*, the region's scrubby, rocky hillsides, provide the best meat options. You'll see rabbit, pigeon, quail, guinea fowl or even wild boar on many a menu. Lamb is the most common of Provençal meats, most often flavoured with rosemary. Among the more daunting dishes count *pieds et paquets*, tripe stuffed with garlic, onions and salt pork, traditionally (although rarely) served with calf's trotters. If you find that difficult to deal with, you may find the idea of *grive* (thrush) pâté or Arles donkey sausage still harder to stomach!

Cherry, apricot and peach orchards make for some of the prettiest of Provençal landscapes. Provençal fruit is fantastic. Fig and almond trees also grow in good number, and their fruits flavour many desserts, as do pine kernels. Provençal *mirabelles*, fresh melons, strawberries and table grapes are all splendid, while the *calissons d'Aix*, with which your meal may end, are a curious Provençal confection, made from a melon and almond paste.

Like Provençal olives, Provençal wine is thought to go back to the Greeks. They're supposed to have introduced one of the principal grape varieties here, syrah (originally grown in Shiraz, Persia), although Provençal wines are notorious for their complicated mix of varieties. To stop you salivating in unseemly fashion as you read on through the culinary and cultural pages that follow, why not open a bottle of complex Châteauneuf-du-Pape, red or white? Or the more sweet-toothed among you could sample a true amber nectar, Muscat de Beaumes-de-Venise. For the tougher palate, opt for a macho aniseed pastis and imagine yourself becoming a village *boules* hero on a Provençal plane-shaded square, or simply lazing on a Provençal restaurant terrace by a cooling, splashing fountain.

Pastis

Lace Wines and Roman Orange

Heading down from Paris to Provence via the infamous road cheerfully known as the Autoroute du Soleil (the Motorway of the Sun), the first major town you come to as you enter modern-day Provence is Orange. Its dusty, traffic-choked streets contain two of the most famous Roman ruins in France, the open-air theatre and the triumphal arch, covered in bizarre, time-worn war sculptures. Orange lies on the flat, just east of the river Rhône, Provence's western frontier. The Rhône—no need to hide it as everyone knows it—has a terrible problem with wind. The *mistral* frequently thunders down the valley, a recurring discomfort.

The best-known and most picturesque of the wine villages of the Ouvèze valley nearby lie at the base of the Dentelles de Montmirail, the 'Lace of Montmirail', a miniature but marvellous mountain range. Its thin dinosaur-like spine of rock makes for a beautiful backdrop to the area, even if in terms of lace it looks dreadfully ragged-edged. Gigondas, Beaumes-de-Venise, Séguret and Sablet are the most famous wine names and wine

Le Mas de Bouvau

villages at the foot of the Dentelles. They also make up a clutch of some of the prettiest villages in Provence. Our restaurant lies on the western side of the valley, totally surrounded by vines, just a few kilometres west of Gigondas, by sleepy little Violès.

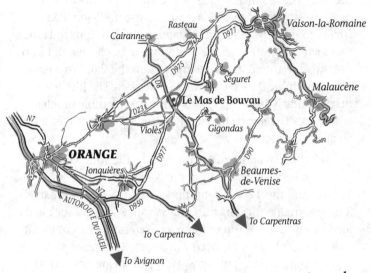

getting there

Violès lies almost due east of Orange. If you're coming south off the A7 motorway take the exit for central Orange. From town, follow the N7 south to Avignon and Carpentras for 7km. You branch off for Carpentras, adopting the D950 for 4km. Then turn off up the D977 towards Vaison-la-Romaine. It's under 8km to Violès. Pass straight through the village. Shortly afterwards, at the crossroads with the D8, head north in the direction of Cairanne. The restaurant's a short way along on the right, among the vines. If you're coming north up the motorway, you can take the exit before Orange by Beaucastel of Châteauneuf-du-Pape fame. Descending the Ouvèze valley from Vaison-la-Romaine, it's easiest to take the road along the south bank of the river out of town, the D977. Before Violès you then turn right up the D8.

Le Mas de Bouvau

Le Mas de Bouvau, Route de Cairanne, 84150 Violès, ✆ 04 90 70 94 08,
✉ 04 90 70 95 99. Closed Sun pm and Mon except in July and Aug. Annual
holidays last week in Aug, 20–30 Dec, and Feb school holidays. Menus at
130F, 195F, 235F and 275F.

A *mas* is a Provençal farm and this one has been converted into a
charming little hotel-cum-restaurant. Lying in the Ouvèze plain, Le
Mas de Bouvau isn't in a spectacular location, but it is prettily and
pretty well swamped by vines. Lines upon lines of them stretch like
waves into the distance. The restaurant not surprisingly boasts an
extremely well chosen wine list. The *mas*'s bulky sides may look a little
battered by the wind, the *mistral* being so common here, but once
through the electric doors installed to keep out the worst gusts, the
place is immaculate.

Three separate dining rooms, each of intimate family size, are laid out
within. One is much brighter than the others, with yellow walls, little
painted Provençal scenes, and windows giving onto an horizon of
vines, rippling into the distance on windy days. There are *santons* too,
the little terracotta Provençal-costumed figures which you may find a
bit of an acquired taste. The most commonly used dining room contains the neat bar and has a big fireplace whose mantelpiece is
decorated with old pots and oil lamps, all giving this room a darker
cosiness. Typical paintings of Provençal countryside by a Parisian
artist, André Pavlowski, decorate the walls, while elegant wine glasses
well suited to wine tasting are set out in readiness for you. Perched on
tall chairs around a tall table, with a crisp tablecloth, fresh flowers and
miniature olives before you, you feel immediately that you're going to
be well looked after. The couple who have created this ambiance and
who prepare and present the refined food are the Hertzogs (a name
from Alsace), a charming pair anxious to please. They speak a
little English as they met each other in London.

Le Mas de Bouvau is one of the best places for you to try
the temptingly named and famed local sweet white wine,
Beaumes-de-Venise, as an *apéritif*. The Château Saint-
Sauveur is not only one of the finest we've ever tasted; it

also has the most appealingly beautiful pink and peachy colour. This Muscat de Beaumes-de-Venise comes from a winemaking family at Aubignan just south of the village of Beaumes-de-Venise and at around 15 per cent volume makes for a heady start to a meal. For those of you who can't stomach sweet white wine, try a glass of a drier local white to whet your appetite. The Domaine Berthet-Rayne Cairanne Côtes-du-Rhône Village 1995 goes down very well.

A glass of Beaumes-de-Venise is seen as *de rigueur* in these parts, however, if you choose the *pâté de foie gras* as your starter. This wickedly luxurious hors d'oeuvre is the compulsory starter for the most expensive of the menus, at 275F, a five-course extravaganza preceded by home-made *tapenade* (the olive paste you'll find spread on toast all over Provence) and a *petite entrée surprise*, a little surprise appetizer. This menu may sound overwhelming, but the cuisine at Le Mas de Bouvau isn't heavy. However, for a much more reasonably priced four-course lunch, you can choose from the 130F menu (not served on Sundays or public holidays). In between these two are menus at 195F and 235F. The 130F menu offers a pretty simple choice, so why not look at a more elaborate one or, rather than going for the four-course menu, decide on three courses *à la carte*, which is a feasible option here.

Duck features strongly among the choices. You might try the duck leg *confit* with orange. The *foie gras* will be of duck, or there's *magret* of duck served with a sauce mixing mustard and Provence honey. Another dish with an interesting sweet touch is the *noisettes d'agneau grillées aux oignons confits*, the delicious onions caramelized in white wine. The pigeon comes from the Lance, an area of isolated hillsides above Nyons in the Drôme provençale. It is amazingly tasty, cooked to perfection (that is, very red), and full of flavour. The pigeon, like the rabbit, which may be prepared in a Côtes-du-Rhône sauce or which you could sample as a starter in the rabbit *rillettes*, is reared on a farm where, as M. Hertzog puts it, these animals have breathed in the flavours of the thyme and other natural herbs. The pigeon, as do the dishes generally, comes with a good selection of vegetables, but it's also accompanied by a finger bowl, which seems to give you permission to use your hands.

The red wine glasses are great, the type into which you can practically put your nose to appreciate to the full the aromas of the local wines. The list from the area is superb. You might be familiar with Gigondas, but why not try a Cairanne from so close to the restaurant, for example the delicious Rabasse Charavin.

Seafood isn't ignored on the menu, most of it actually supplied from the west of France. Among the most interesting fish dishes is the salmon smoked at Le Mas de Bouvau using *sarments de vigne*, vine shoots, served with olive oil perfumed with herbs. Or what about *suprême de pintade aux huitres*, guinea fowl with oysters?

The cheese trolley includes a wide range of French cheeses, but it's hard to beat the thin slice of buttery *brebis*, ewe's milk cheese, served with a light salad laced with walnut oil. Or try the goat's cheese with *marc*. You'll probably have been distracted by the pudding trolley rattling temptingly around the dining room by the time it comes to your turn to choose from it. Generally there's a large range of tarts, on our last visit plum tart, pear tart, orange tart and lemon tart, possibly served with a raspberry *coulis*. What was described as a *tarte au citron* was more like a lovely light lemon mousse served on pastry, while the *mousse au chocolat* was the real thing, rich and melting. Pieces of nuts added to the texture of the orange tart, which was sprinkled with ground almonds, while the chocolate mousse had a hint of orange flavouring.

Pigeons de la Lance Rôti Crème d'Ail

Serve this dish with gratin dauphinois and a red wine—Vacqueyras 1990 is recommended.

Serves 6

3 pigeons or quail, each approximately 450–750g/1–1½lbs
salt and pepper
3 tablespoons olive oil
4 tablespoons marc de Provence or brandy

For the sauce:

1 litre/1¾ pints water
1 garlic bulb
2 tablespoons olive oil
1 small potato, peeled and diced
1 heaped tablespoon thick crème fraîche

Preheat the oven to 230° or 240°C/450° or 475°F (gas mark 8 or 9). Clean out the pigeons or quail. Season inside and out. Place them in a roasting dish and sprinkle the 3 tablespoons of olive oil over them. Cook in the pre-heated oven for 20 to 30 minutes. Your pigeons are cooked if, when you prick the breasts with a fork, the juice which runs out is pinkish in colour. Next, flambé the pigeons in marc de Provence.

To make the sauce, bring the water to the boil, peel the garlic and cook the cloves in the water. Season with salt and pepper and add the 2 tablespoons of olive oil. Keep the water boiling. Add the diced potato and cook for 30 minutes. Put the sauce into a blender and blend well. Then add the crème fraîche. Return the sauce to the pan and cook until it has reduced and is a creamy consistency. Adjust the seasoning to taste.

To serve, cut each of the pigeons or quail in half and serve the sauce separately.

---

touring around

It's probably best to visit **Orange** in the morning before the pollution has had time to clog up the air too much and as you probably won't want too strenuous an afternoon after a lunch at the Mas de Bouvau.

Rome took good care of its soldiers; keeping its word by them was one secret of the empire's success. Nine years after Julius Caesar's death, many veterans of the Second Gallic Legion were ready for their promised retirement. The pattern was already set. Rome would establish a colony for them in the lands they conquered, often replacing a native village they had destroyed. The colony that became Orange was called *Colonia Julia Secundanorum Arausio*.

The architects of Orange's **Théâtre Antique** (*open daily 9–6.30 in summer, 9–12.30 and 1.30–5 in winter, guided tours July and August only;*

adm; also valid for Municipal Museum) might be distressed to hear it, but these days the most impressive part of this huge structure is its back wall. 'The best wall in my kingdom', Louis XIV is said to have called it. Built in the early 1st century AD, the theatre is a testimony to the culture and wealth of *Arausio*. Like the Colosseum in Rome, it even had a massive awning (*velum*), a contraption of canvas and beams that could be raised to cover most of the spectators. All over the Mediterranean, theatres fell into disuse in the cultural degradation of the late Roman empire. This one was probably already abandoned when it burned in the 4th or 5th century. In the Middle Ages other buildings grew up over the ruins; old prints show the semicircular tiers of seats (*cavea*) half-filled in and covered with ramshackle houses.

Unlike Greek theatres, which always opened to a grand view behind the stage, those of the Romans featured large stage buildings, serious architectural compositions of columns, arches and sculptured friezes. This is what the great exterior wall is supporting; Orange's stage building (35m high) is one of only two complete specimens that remain to us (the other is at Aspendos, in Turkey), though the fragments of its decoration are mostly in the municipal museum across the street. A statue of Augustus remains, in the centre, over an inscription honouring the people of *Arausio* and welcoming them to the show.

Save some time for the bulging curiosity shop of the **Musée Municipal** (*open daily 9–7 in summer, 9–12 and 1.30–5.30 in winter; adm*), directly opposite the theatre on Place des Frères-Mounet; it is one of the most fascinating town museums in Provence. As expected, the main rooms are given over to Roman art, including an exceptional frieze of satyrs and amazons from the theatre. The *plan cadastral* (land survey) is unique: a stone tablet engraved with property records for the broad Roman grid of farmland between Orange and Montélimar. The first pieces of it were discovered in 1856, though no one guessed what they were until the rest turned up, between 1927 and 1954; since then they have been a great aid to scholars in filling in some of the everyday details of Roman life and law.

Climbing the stairs into the upper levels of the museum, you'll pass rooms of Dutch portraits and relics of Nassau rule—Orange as a result

the triumphal arch Orange

lent its colour to the Dutch, the Northern Irish, the Orange Free State and Orange, New Jersey—and a collection of works by the Welsh impressionist Frank Brangwyn (who was, in fact, born in Bruges): heroic compositions among wharves and factories, along with some lovely country scenes. The most unexpected exhibit is the Salle des Wetters, a remarkable relic of the Industrial Revolution in France. The Wetters were a family of mid-18th-century industrialists who produced *indiennes*, printed cotton cloth much in demand at the time. They commissioned an artist named G. M. Rossetti to paint a record of their business; this he did (in 1764) in incredible detail, on five huge, colourful naive canvases showing every aspect of the making of *indiennes*, from the stevedores unloading the cotton on the docks to the shy, serious factory girls in the great hall.

Rue Victor Hugo, roughly following the route of the ancient Roman main street, or *cardo major*, is the axis that leads to Orange's other famed Roman attraction. The **Triumphal Arch**, built around 20 AD, celebrates the conquests of the Second Gallic Legion with outlandish, almost abstract scenes of battling Romans and Celts. This is the epitome of the Provençal-Roman style: excellent, careful reliefs, especially in the upper frieze, portraying a naval battle, though with a touch of Celto-Ligurian strangeness in the details. Odd oval shields are a prominent feature, decorated with heraldic devices and thunderbolts. Seemingly random symbols at the upper left—a whip, a pitcher, something that looks like a bishop's crozier, and others—are in fact symbols of animal sacrifice and marine attributes (the 'crozier' is the prow of a ship). On the sides of the arch are heaps of arms—

'triumphs'—that were to influence the militaristic art fostered by rulers such as Emperor Charles V in the Renaissance. A little over a half-century before this arch was built, Orange was still Rome's wild frontier, and art such as this evokes it vividly.

Make the most of the afternoon to discover the pretty **wine territory** around Le Mas de Bouvau. First, some recommendations for visits to wine estates from the proprietors of the restaurant themselves. If you appreciated a particular wine over lunch, why not ask the Hertzogs where the domain is to be found and how easy it would be to visit it. For instance, the other side of Violès from the restaurant, down towards Jonquières along the D977, the Château de Malijay is one welcoming local address where the winery comes with an extremely elegant-looking country home and where a series of concerts is organized in the early months of the year. The restaurant's Cairanne selection is particularly good, so you could ask about the possibility of going to Corinne Coturier's Rabasse Charavin or M. Alary's Oratoire St-Martin.

One of our favourite Beaumes-de-Venise has already been mentioned. Take the D8 south from Le Mas de Bouvau and you can go to have a look around the village of **Beaumes-de-Venise** itself at the southern end of the Dentelles de Montmirail and discover other estates there. The *vin doux naturel*, the sweet white of Beaumes-de-Venise made from the muscat grape, isn't entirely natural. It's made by partially fermenting very ripe grapes and arresting the fermentation by the addition of alcohol which kills off the yeasts, leaving much of the sugar and giving the wine an extra potency. The locals find the rather eccentric Anglo-Saxon habit of treating the wine as a dessert drink highly amusing as they take it as an *apéritif*.

Above the local cooperative lies the Romanesque church of Notre-Dame d'Aubune, its tall bell tower embellished with later classical pilasters and set against the first southern slopes of the Dentelles. Head up the narrow roads through the rocky countryside to the church. You could then follow the track up the *Côte balméenne*, its ancient terraces concealing the signs of 5000 years of civilization. Panels explain that Greeks, Celto-Ligurians, Romans and Saracens settled here at various periods through history. Since the late 1980s the terraces have been replanted with olive, almond and fruit trees, as well as caper shrubs. The *sentier botanique* or botanical walk leads you through Mediterranean vegetation typical of the Provençal *garrigues*.

Continue to **Gigondas** itself, star of the wine villages and *appellations* in the area. The main street of wine boutiques is crammed with merry *dégustateurs* in high season. The very name of Gigondas apparently derives from joy, or *jocunditas*, after a holiday camp for Roman soldiers established on the spot. Gigondas produces one of the most subtle, noble, dark and fragrant of all Côtes-du-Rhônes. In the centre of the village, the Syndicat des Vins is a useful place to start tasting and selecting estates, as it represents almost 50 of them. By contrast the cooperative Cave des Vignerons de Gigondas amalgamates some 20 per cent of the *appellation*'s production, such generic wines as their Signature and Pavillon de Beaumirail worth considering. Among the estate-produced wines, the Domaine Les Pallières in Gigondas is the headquarters from which the late M. Roux led his dynamic and successful campaign to encourage his fellow producers to concentrate on high quality.

To clear your mind for a moment in the midst of all this head-spinning reflection on alcohol, you could take an invigorating walk or a steep drive up the Gigondas hillside. Follow the signs east out of the village and tracks lead you into the Dentelles from which, after the fairly strenuous climb, you're rewarded with spectacular views down onto the great Ouvèze vineyard valley where you ate.

Sablet is the village north of Gigondas, not as glamorous, but still pretty, its houses tightly packed on its rounded, ramparted hillock, like an island the vines haven't been able to inundate. Sablet has an unpretentious charm, its covered alleys known as *soustets*. In the centre there's a Caveau des Vignerons. Many fine wine estates lie around the village, such as the Domaine Piaugier, run by Jean-Marc Autran, actually the youthful superstar of Gigondas, but who produces reputed Sablet wines too. One of the finest wine estates of the area that we've visited regularly is the Château du Trignon, where you can try an excellent selection of Rhône wines.

Finish the day at **Séguret**, most picturesque of all the area's villages, clinging to the side of the Dentelles, the tower of a medieval castle high above it. You can't drive into the village but have to leave your car in one of the car parks just outside it. Despite being officially designated one of the *plus beaux villages de France* by the association of that name, Séguret hasn't been ruined by tourism. Walk along the cobbled main street with its crafts boutiques to the delightful plane-shaded square at the eastern end, the knobbly branches deliberately knotted together to provide a shading roof. The village is a good base for hiking. It lies along two official trails (GR4 and GR7) and there's a village track that passes through a gap in the Dentelles to the eastern side.

Back with things culinary, at the top of the village you'll find La Table du Comtat, a well-known, highly-reputed hotel and restaurant. If you've worked up another appetite in the afternoon, you could try it for dinner. Or you could settle for the simpler but charming terrace of Le Mesclun, a restaurant on the main street that we've often enjoyed eating at, in an idyllic spot where you could simply stop to appreciate the views out over the slopes of the Dentelles de Montmirail, inebriated, we hope, by the happiness of the day.

Cobblers to a New Restaurant in Vaison-la-Romaine

With the Mont Ventoux threatening in the middle distance, Vaison-la-Romaine, squashed into the valley of the Ouvèze river, has practically seen it all in terms of Provençal civilization…and a surprising amount of it survives. The crooked streets up to the abandoned medieval castle ruins and the ever-so-neatly restored Roman remains are two excellent reasons to visit this vibrant town.

Le Brin d'Olivier

To most French people, however, Vaison's name is associated with a terrible recent tragedy. The Ouvèze valley tightens here to form a gorge, and one wet September night in 1992 a mass of water built up such force and fury that thirty people were drowned or carried away to their deaths, and the damage was appalling. For a time normally bright Vaison became a dismally depressed place. It also became something of a symbol of the dangers of the corruption of French local politicians, as it was revealed that some of the houses that were destroyed had been built on land where construction was supposed to have been prohibited.

From Vaison, you could easily follow the wine villages route suggested in the first chapter, only in reverse (see pp.9–10). Here we propose a day sticking to the city's rich sites and just a quick trip to the spectacular *village perché* or hilltop village of Crestet a short distance to the south.

getting there

Vaison-la-Romaine lies in a northern corner of the *département* of Vaucluse, northwest of the Mont Ventoux. Tucked away down a short street by the river, Le Brin d'Olivier is well positioned between the old and the new town. Park on the spacious car park on the west side of the Ouvèze river, by the old Roman bridge. (A plaque on the house with a tower whose roof carries green-glazed tiles notes in Provençal that 'l'ou poeto Teodor Aubanel' wrote the *Venus d'Arles* of Félibrige fame here.) The little street on which the restaurant stands is very close to the Roman bridge. Look out for green gates and the courtyard entrance to the restaurant.

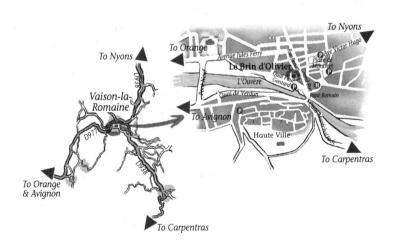

Le Brin d'Olivier

Le Brin d'Olivier, 4 Rue du Ventoux, 84110 Vaison-la-Romaine, © 04 90 28 74 79. Closed Wed and Sat lunch. Holidays one week end June/early July, last week of Nov and first fortnight Dec. Menus at 70F, 120F, 150F and 180F.

Once occupied by cobblers, this old tonhouse has been converted into a restaurant by a very young couple getting off to an admirable start in the restaurant business. The place had gone to rack and ruin, neglected some 30 years, when Olivia and Didier Rogne bought it in December 1994. The downstairs now houses the kitchen and a couple of small dining rooms while the newlyweds (they allowed themselves ten days off to get married in June 1996) live upstairs. You can also eat in the private little courtyard.

There's definitely something a touch romantic now about Le Brin d'Olivier. Rather than being a brash modern transformation, it hides discreetly behind its large green metallic portal. This opens onto the lovely enclosed courtyard with an olive tree at its centre (*le brin d'olivier* means the twig of an olive tree), lavender growing at its feet. Along with the plants in pots, the dried flowers, the decorative bird cages and ox yolks, the strange funnel-shaped object that may draw your attention in the courtyard was once used to unravel silk cocoons. Part of the courtyard is covered, while a little alcove is reserved for a table for two. This restaurant, inside and out, is an intimate place.

In the first dining room, a frieze of olive branch decoration runs like a waistband around the room. We ate in the second, under dried hydrangea and beams hacked by innumerable little cuts. It looks as though an axe-murderer has been let loose on these for a little light therapy...or perhaps a crazed cook. Rest assured, however, that Olivia, the chef here, in her mid-20s, seems very much in control. Before starting up this restaurant, she worked at one of the best-known gastronomic addresses in the Vaucluse, La Table du Comtat in nearby Séguret.

'Trendy Provençal' might be a suitable description for the cooking, with herbs aplenty in most dishes, including the puddings. But the overriding feeling that comes across is a care for detail, in the food as well as the decoration. The only jarring note was the music being pumped out too loudly into the small space.

Once you've untied the straw that amusingly encircles your napkin, you can contemplate the menus. For those trying to keep to a tight budget, the 70F lunchtime *déjeuner sur le pouce* (a French idiom meaning a quick bite to eat—not served Sundays or public holidays) represents a bargain, maybe consisting of an aubergine mousse or salad of little blinis with *tapenade* to start with, followed by the dish of the day, then pudding or *faisselle* (a kind of fromage blanc that's very popular in Provence—the word more generally means a cheese strainer). The menu is excellent value for this standard of cooking.

None of the menus is particularly expensive though, especially given the care taken over them. The *menu d'ici* ('menu from around here') comes at 120F, the top *menu aux senteurs de Provence* ('menu of the scents of Provence') at 180F—both offering four courses. With the *menu malin* ('the crafty menu') for 150F you can pick and choose between the dishes of the two other main menus.

Great attention has even been paid to the selection of the plates for each dish. Some are white, their edges embossed with little angels, others of glass, with *fleurs de lys* and floral motifs, others still surrounded by hearts, or with fish all over them. Before the starters arrived, we were served a little *amuse-gueule* or appetizer of cockles. Most of us tried a Mont Ventoux wine with the hors d'oeuvre, a Domaine de St-Claude Blanc de Blancs Côtes-du-Rhône 1994—nicely dry, crisp and appley. The starters go from the well seasoned to the pretty spicy. The mussels risotto with thyme were peppery, served in a very tasty sauce. The original spring rolls actually turned out to be marinated salmon wrapped in large slices of aubergines—the little velvet swimming crab as decoration gave away that the dish was fairly salty. On the more expensive menu the ravioli with a creamy truffle sauce went down particularly well, very nutty in taste, while the *terrine de foie gras* marinated in Rasteau (the sweet variety) came with *pain aux épices*.

Portions for the main courses are very generous, with plenty of sauces where relevant. Among the choice of main courses, a good selection of vegetables accompanied the *aïoli de cabillaud*, notably courgettes, potatoes and beans, the *aïoli* probably with enough garlic for the average Englishman's week. Delicious. Still better was the *ail en chemise* (whole cloves of garlic cooked in their skins) that starred with the *magret de canard à l'ail, petite ratatouille*, the garlic here more nutty, even chestnutty, in taste than garlicky. The sharp, shark-like knife that was supplied to tackle the *magret de canard* was a reminder that this dish can be a bit chewy, but the meat was pink, served on a vast bed of tasty *ratatouille* that would only have appeared *petite* to a giant. The fresh pasta to accompany the peppered steak was flavoured with basil, the salmon steak with a basil butter sauce, the lamb with thyme flowers.

Those who opt for red wine could try La Fiole du Chevalier d'Elbène—it sounds like something out of Arthurian legend—, a Séguret 1989. It has been *élevé en fût de chêne*, that is, aged in oak barrels. Along with its deep blackcurrant colour it smells of cherries, but has an earthy more than a fruity taste, which probably has something to do with that oak.

The cheese dishes are mercifully modest in size. You can choose between a half little goat's cheese on a bed of red lettuce and *faisselle* pepped up by a *coulis* or sauce of red fruits. In contrast, most of the puddings are more complex, each one seemingly flavoured with a different herb. The *crème brûlée* came with rosemary—there were actual pieces of it in the pudding—,the red fruits in sauce with mint, the chocolate *parfait* with a verbena cream. The last pudding was delicious, a perfect melting compromise between a chocolate mousse and a chocolate truffle. Watch out, though, that you don't break your teeth on the *croquantes à la fleur d'orange*, which could potentially end the meal in the wrong way. Coffee was served with these and other 'mouse cakes', as one guest described the *petits fours*!

Tapenade

Try this spread on grilled croûtons—this is the great Provençal appetizer.
Makes 1 small jarful

300g/10¾ oz black olives, stoned
3 garlic cloves
thyme
pepper, to taste
2 tablespoons olive oil

Place all the ingredients in a food processor and
purée. Store in a clean screw-topped jar and use within 1–2 weeks.

---

touring around

Vaison began on the heights south of the Ouvèze as a Celtic *oppidum*. In the late 2nd century BC, the Romans took control and refounded it as *Vasio Vocontiorum* and it prospered spectacularly for the next five centuries. In the 1300s Vaison fell into the hands of the pope, along with the rest of the Comtat Venaissin, a separate county that once covered a large slice of this part of Provence, remaining independent from the French crown, and not becoming part of France until the Revolution. In 1840, the first excavations were undertaken in the Roman city. Vaison nevertheless had to wait for a local cleric, the Abbé Sautel, to do the job seriously. He dug from 1907 until 1955, financed mostly by a local businessman.

The Abbé uncovered almost 11 hectares of Roman Vaison's foundations, while the modern town grew up around the digs. There are two separate areas, the Quartier de la Villasse and the Quartier de Puymin; their entrances are on either side of the central Place Abbé Sautel, by the Tourist Information pavilion. Vaison's **ruins** (*open daily 10–12 and 2–4.30, closed Tues in winter; 9–12 and 2–6.45 in summer; same adm for both, also includes cathedral cloister*) are an argument for leaving the archaeologists alone; with everything sanitized and tidy, interspersed with gardens and playgrounds, there is the unmistakable air of an archaeological theme park. The Villasse is the smaller of the two areas; from the entrance, a Roman street takes you past the city's baths (the best parts are still hidden under Vaison's post office) and the Maison au Buste d'Argent, a truly posh villa with two *atria* and some mosaic floors. It has its own baths, as does the adjacent Maison au Dauphin; beyond this is a short stretch of a colonnaded street, a status embellishment in the most prosperous Roman towns.

The Puymin quarter has more of the same: another villa, the Maison des Messii, is near the entrance. Beyond that, however, is an *insula*, or block of flats for the common folk, as well as a large, partially excavated quadrangle called the Portique de Pompée, an enclosed public garden with statuary that was probably attached to a temple. On the opposite side of the *insula* is a much-ruined *nymphaeum*, or monumental fountain. From here you can walk uphill to the theatre, restored and used for concerts in the summer, and the museum, displaying the best of the finds from the excavations. You'll learn more about Roman Vaison here than from the bare foundations around it; there's a model of one of the villas as it may have looked. All the items a Roman museum must have are present: restored mosaics and fragments of wall painting, some lead pipes, inscriptions, hairpins and bracelets, and of course statuary: municipal notables of Vaison, a wonderful monster *acroterion* (roof ornament) from a mausoleum, and a few marble gods and emperors—including a startling family portrait with the Emperor Hadrian completely naked and evidently proud of

olive stall

it, next to his demurely clothed Empress Sabina, smiling wanly.

From Roman and modern Vaison, the medieval version of the town is a splendid sight atop its cliff, a honey-coloured skyline of stone houses under the castle of the Counts of Toulouse. Almost abandoned at the turn of the century, the **Haute-Ville** is becoming quite chic now, with restorations everywhere and more than a few artists' studios. You reach it by crossing the Ouvèze on the Roman bridge, still in good nick after 18 centuries of service, a survivor of the terrible 1992 flood. Climb up to the gate of the 14th-century fortifications, next to the Tour Beffroi, the clock-tower which is the most prominent sight of the Haute-Ville's silhouette. The cobbled streets and the shady Place du Vieux Marché with its fountain are lovely; trails lead higher up to the 12th- to 14th-century castle, much of it destroyed but offering a view and a good opportunity to clamber round rocks and ruins.

Crestet is perched on, well, a crest, on the heights above the D938 to Malaucène, some four kilometres from Vaison. It's an eagle's eerie of a village. Clearly abandoned at one stage, several of the houses in the centre remain mere shells. Others have been done up as holiday homes. The views from the terrace by the church onto the fruit-filled valley below and the mountains in the distance are elevating. To the north, you can normally make out the Baronnies range, while much closer and to the east rises the Mont Ventoux.

In the pine-scented forest some way out from the village, the Crestet Centre d'Art (*free to visit*) feels splendidly lost in the middle of nowhere. Spaces both within and outside the straight lines and shapes of the modern house built by the architect Bruno Stahy are devoted to modern exhibitions. Pieces of outdoor sculpture might surprise you on your walk: a great Calder-like mobile, a metal dinosaur bird moving in the breeze; or Pat Bruder's version of the tomb from Poussin's *Et in Arcadia Ego*. The shepherds in the original point to the sarcophagus, symbol of the presence of mortality even in the bliss of Arcady. The tomb here is actually of openwork, with Meccano-like snakes serpenting around. One of the major displays inside was suitably culinary when we last went, the work of Michel Blazy, a *projet d'intérieur agréable aux insectes* (project for an interior agreeable to insects). A room was decorated with various piles of decomposing food, the idea seemingly to find out how insects and nature more generally reacted. A potato was set majestically on a macaroni pedestal, tomatoes were left hanging from stalactites of glue, a circle of puréed carrots had been left on the floor to see what mould and which little flies might be attracted. Whatever the divided opinions on the varied pieces of art, no one complained about the views.

The Great Windy One

Bedoin

Bald-headed Mont Ventoux (you could translate that as Mount Windy) is one of the great characters of Provence's landscape, the Vaucluse's dominant personality, the most majestic old mountain in the northwest of the region. It's so tree-deprived up top that even in the height of summer it looks snow-capped. Despite the name, it has dignity and seems to have been considered sacred by the Celts.

Malaucène, a lively, large village at the bottom of the Windy One's western slopes, is generally the starting point for a trip up the mountain, whether you're walking, cycling or driving. It's from here that the great 14th-century poet, cleric and scholar Petrarch made his famous ascent in 1336, often described as Europe's first recorded piece of mountain-climbing for the hell of it. Petrarch wrote of the experience in correspondence with a dear friend. It's a powerful, moving little letter showing a man setting out to satisfy a long-held desire without imagining beforehand that the physical ascent might give rise to deep soul-searching about the difficulties of a Christian's moral ascent through life.

For us a trip up the Mont Ventoux should be a little less stressful than for Petrarch, the lunch at La Maison hopefully not leading to too profound a moral crisis. But remember that the mountain bears its name well. If the wind is blowing too strongly the day you go to La Maison, you'd do better to make do with a tour round the delightful villages at the Mont Ventoux's feet, several producing palatable little wines. Many of the villages in the Windy One's shadow have magical countryside and views around them.

getting there

Go to Malaucène, south from Vaison-la-Romaine along the D938, or north from Carpentras on the same road. On Malaucène's boulevard of plane trees, look out carefully for the signs to Beaumont-du-Ventoux. There was no road up the mountain in Petrarch's day, nor in fact until this century. He had to pick his own path, and it appears possible that he set off along the valley in which our enchanting restaurant for the day is to be found. A shepherd he met along the valley tried to dissuade Petrarch from embarking on his foolish escapade, warning that it would end in tears. Mme. Rozenblat, who runs La Maison, has kindly put up little signs counting down the few kilometres to Beaumont-du-Ventoux to reassure you that you aren't getting lost on the way to her restaurant, as it's a slightly longer country road ride than you might expect. The countdown helps whet the appetite.

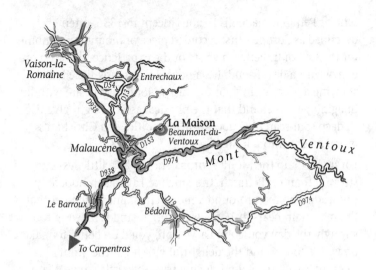

La Maison

La Maison, Pierlaud, Hameau de Piolon, 84340 Beaumont-du-Ventoux,
✆ and ✉ 04 90 65 15 50. Closed July and Aug Mon and Tues lunchtimes;
out of season Mon and Tues; and Oct–Easter. Menu at 140F plus, from
1997, one at 110F.

La Maison is a misleading name for this restaurant. Its simplicity
doesn't make you expect the stylish, sophisticated address that awaits
you practically in the middle of nowhere. What's more, in summer
most of the action takes place not in the house, but outside, on the
splendid split-level paved courtyard. And finally, this courtyard is surrounded by charming buildings on three sides—this doesn't look like
an ordinary house at all, but like a farmyard. It's been delightfully
done up by Mme. Rozenblat, who also has a couple of rooms you can
stay at. The deceptive feel is that you're on a little village square. The
village and location look lovely, the ugly brute of a *cave coopérative* the
jarring note.

You'll immediately forget about that under the lime trees providing
shade for La Maison's square, together with a panoply of parasols over

the numerous white metallic tables and chairs set out around it. Herbs grow healthily against the walls. Water flows into a trough. One table more private than the rest is placed in what was formally a shed.

Actually we didn't eat here on a warm summer lunchtime, but on a rainy September evening. The snails had come out in force to enjoy the wet weather. Mme. Rozenblat seemed most concerned about them; we weren't sure whether it was out of charitable concern for their well-being or because she felt they should be kept intact for the pot. Mme. Rozenblat is certainly a very gentle host, and the bright yellow interior was heartwarming given the weather. You walk into two interconnecting rooms, the first containing a table with a pile of books and magazines about Provence and the Mont Ventoux, the second the dining room. In the dining room with its half-dozen tables, a couple of *objets d'art* stand on the mantelpiece above the stone chimney. A lamp embellished with a print block for decorating material draws the attention, as does a cloisonné pastel painting of the Mont Ventoux. Opera was playing in the background. Here the feeling is definitely homely and warm, especially with the thick cream curtains drawn.

There was only one menu in 1996, but a wide choice for each course, and four courses of good cuisine for 140F is a bargain. Or you can choose *à la carte*. In 1997 there's a 110F menu too. The cooking is classic stuff, as refined as the surroundings. Provençal dishes feature of course, but one or two touches, such as the *compote de gésiers de canard en gelée* and the *cuisse de canard en confit* hint at an influence from the southwest of France, and that indeed is where the chef, Raymond Lardiès, stems from.

A greyish, slightly nutty-tasting *tapenade* is served as you make your choice. There wasn't anything wildly original about the selection of hors d'oeuvre, but from the start the food was well executed. The *tarte saumonée à l'émincé de poireaux* was light and delicate in taste. The sardines, marinated in white wine and very flavoursome, were presented on a trencher. If you like gizzard then its texture is interestingly contrasted with that of the bed of lentils on which the pieces are served. Or you could opt for reassuring old favourites such as tomato and mozzarella salad with basil, melon with Parma ham, or *aubergines confites*.

Of the main courses, the *pintadeau en croûte* was particularly good. You had the satisfaction of breaking through the nicely cooked crust of this guinea fowl pie and then waiting a while for the stew inside to cool as the aromas wafted out. There was a generous selection of vegetables mixed in with the meat. *Pieds et paquets* are an acquired taste, but one diner at our table pigged himself with delight.

The *magret de canard* was accompanied by slightly sweet, soft and melting *oignons confits*. You had to pay a small supplement for this addition, as you did for the seasonal fungi, trumpet and morel mushrooms, which accompanied other dishes.

Mme. Rozenblat has cleverly invested in some older Vaucluse vintages, so we tried a delicious Cairanne 1985, showing how well wines from that region can age. The French tend to drink them younger. If you want something more modest to accompany your meal, you could try the results from that ugly cooperative outside.

The main courses were filling; the *faisselle*, though fresh, was still more so as it was bathing in cream. You could opt for a little Drôme goat's cheese instead. For dessert you might find the *colonel* cleansing, lime sorbet served with vodka. Or the seasonal fruits refreshing. One level richer, you might choose between a *nougat glacé* and a *vacherin glacé framboise cassis*. The *chausson aux pêches tièdes*, peaches in warm pastry, was still quite light, as was the *tarte à la rhubarbe meringuée*, but for those who don't find the weight of a meal a problem there should be old favourites such as vanilla *crème brûlée* and *fondant au chocolat* with a *crème anglaise* containing grains of coffee.

Aubergines à la Provençale

Serves 4

4 medium-sized aubergines

For the sauce:
1 onion, finely chopped
1 red pepper, finely chopped

1 green pepper, finely chopped
1 garlic clove, finely chopped
1 tablespoon olive oil
6 tablespoons tomato purée
1 litre/1 ¾ pints chicken stock
4 sprigs thyme
salt and pepper

To serve:

½ iceberg or other crisp, green lettuce, leaves washed, drained and trimmed

Wash the aubergines. Take a sharp knife and make an incision on one side of each aubergine, piercing the skin and flesh. Fry the aubergines quickly. Remove and leave to drain overnight.

Preheat the oven to 150°C/300°F (gas mark 2). To make the sauce, sweat the onions, peppers and garlic in the olive oil until soft. Add the tomato purée, stock, thyme and salt and pepper. Cook for about 15 minutes.

Arrange the aubergines in an ovenproof dish with the pierced sides up. Fill the aubergines with sauce. Pour the rest of the sauce around them. Bake in the preheated oven for 1 ½ hours. Remove the aubergines from the oven and leave them to cool.

Serve garnished with the crisp green lettuce.

touring around

On a day devoted to the **Mont Ventoux**, you should really wake before dawn to read your Petrarch by candle light (original Latin text optional; the French translation of the letter relating his climb goes by the religious-sounding title of the *Ascension du Mont-Ventoux*). Then head out at first light for the summit to make the most of the clear morning air and to avoid the buses packed with tourists as well as the very foolhardy cyclists who struggle up the slopes in great number. Tragically, people do die taking on this old tourist war horse—a memorial on the Ventoux's eastern road is dedicated to the British cyclist Tommy Simpson who succumbed during one Tour de France.

The black and yellow poles on the roadside indicate that there can be heavy snow up here in winter. You even pass the Mont Ventoux's little ski resort on the way up. Fighter planes may flit around you at most alarming speed.

At the top of the Mont Ventoux, the views can be elating. To the north you can make out the Baronnies and the foothills of the Alps in the Drôme. To the northeast you can see some of the major peaks of the Alps themselves, the soaring spiky-tipped mountains described to us as the Massif des Ecrins by a man who seemed to know. To the east are the Alps leading to Italy—check the names on the orientation table. To the south lies the Mediterranean, or at least views onto the Lubéron; to the west, the now diminutive-looking Dentelles de Montmirail and the Rhône valley. The building marking the summit looks like something transported from New York. There's a peculiar proliferation of sweet sellers up here, their artificially coloured confections glinting in the crystal light like some gawdy, otherwordly gems.

Petrarch described his astonishment on the summit nicely: '...surprised by the strangely light air and the grandiose spectacle, I stood there as though stupefied. I looked behind me; the clouds were at my feet and I began to believe in the reality of Mount Athos and Mount Olympus...'. At 2911m, Mount Olympus is almost exactly 1000m higher than the Mont Ventoux, but the spikes of Les Ecrins reach the dizzy 3500m mark. Another statistic to warn you about—the *mistral* can blow at up to 250km an hour up here. On such extreme occasions the road up to the top will be shut, but you should be aware that on many days the Windy One more than lives up to its name.

If you did get up quite early, you could descend via the eastern side of the mountain and follow the D974 along the Ventoux's southern flank to **Bédoin**. The path from around this village is supposed to be the nicest walking way up the Mont Ventoux.

After lunch, what about a light stroll to go and see the tracks of the former **Roman road** that passed so close to Beaumont-du-Ventoux? Mme. Rozenblat can give you instructions on how to get to the ancient way, the grooves worn into the stone by the carts' wheels still visible. Nowadays this place is really off the beaten track. Cherry trees grow in large numbers in this fertile valley. As a Parisian who has retreated here, Mme. Rozenblat calls this part of the country *le bout du monde*, the end of the earth, and you do feel quite detached from the stress of modern civilization. Mme. Rozenblat can also tell you a little about the beautiful string of Romanesque chapels across the *commune* of Beaumont-du-Ventoux. The little Ste-Marguerite is especially beautiful. The area seems to have inspired reflection and apparently women who chose to retreat into convent life came in particularly large numbers.

Malaucène itself has a couple of religious curiosities, its landmark church of St-Michel-et-St-Pierre built in 1309 by Pope Clement V. The D974 out of town passes a pre-Celtic site dedicated not to wind but to water. Notre-Dame-du-Groseau marks the spot today, an unusual 11th-century octagonal chapel. Originally this was part of a large monastery, now vanished. Clement V used it as his summer home, and his escutcheon can be seen painted inside (the priest at Malaucène has the key). But this was also a holy spot in remotest antiquity; the iron cross outside the chapel is planted on a stone believed to have been a Celtic altar. Groseau derives from the name Groselos, a Celtic god of springs; the object of veneration is a short distance up the road, the Source du Groseau, pouring out of a cliff face. The Romans, as they did at Fontaine-de-Vaucluse, channelled the spring into an aqueduct for the city of Vaison. Fragments of this can still be seen.

To view some spectacular scenery without the hassle of the winding roads and wind of the Ventoux if the *mistral* is blowing too violently, head back into Malaucène, and at the northern exit from the village going towards Vaison, turn onto the little road to Suzette in the Dentelles de Montmirail. This is the kind of road along which everyone inevitably sighs out loud at the beauty of the scenery, lost for words. At Suzette, you can head for **Le Barroux**, whose castle peering out from the wooded hills you should have spotted several times by now. This 13-century structure belonged to the lords of Les Baux at one time—they loved hide-outs in impregnable positions. Prince Charles of the present beleaguered British royal family has apparently appreciated it too, for a holiday.

A Fashionable Dash of Colour in Carpentras

Les Rives d'Auzon

Carpentras is fairly centrally located in the Vaucluse *département*, but remains out of the Provence limelight, despite being an appealing town. Its couple of arcades protect a diversity of boutiques among its curious attractions, most notable of which is the cathedral.

For a busy touristic or shopping afternoon, take the road straight south from Carpentras, which leads to the many-fountained charms of Pernes-les-Fontaines and to the island of antique dealers at L'Isle-sur-la Sorgue. The Sorgue is the river which begins so dramatically at the Fontaine-de-Vaucluse nearby, one of the major tourist sites and natural wonders of Provence.

getting there

Les Rives d'Auzon stands out vibrantly on the main ring road of a boulevard that encircles the old town of Carpentras, opposite the great tooth-crenellated main gateway into town, the Porte d'Orange. Watch out, this many-laned ring road is a danger. Once you're on it you can feel like you're caught on a fast-spinning merry-go-round, and merry-go-rounds only go round one way, of course. But you should be able to spot Les Rives d'Auzon's ox-blood-red façade and yellow details fairly easily. If you can't park on the side of the boulevard itself, just after passing in front of the restaurant you can take a right turn down into the steep town ditch where there's a well-signposted large public car park. The town authorities have even installed an outdoor lift to take you back up from here to the old town.

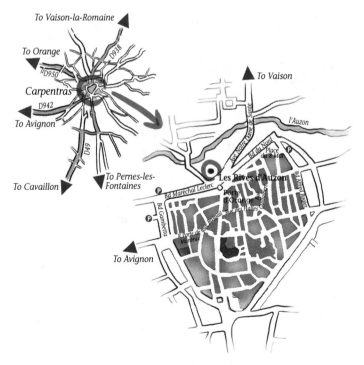

Les Rives d'Auzon

*Les Rives d'Auzon, 47 Boulevard du Nord, 84200 Carpentras, ℗ 04 90 60
62 62. Closed Mon and Sat lunchtimes and Sun. Menus at 85F, 110F (these
two only at lunchtimes), 130F and 158F.*

Issey Miyake eat your heart out. The Japanese fashion designer would
probably be in seventh heaven seeing all this distressed, crumpled,
silken material spread so generously over the tables at Les Rives
d'Auzon. After the restaurant's bold exterior, the colours of the double
dining room also deliberately startle. Lavender mauve or gold for the
tablecloths, green and red for the large summer chairs in wide plaited
cane like thick bands of pasta, grass-green for the table mats, a very
deep red for the generous wine rack. Even the loo paper is worth going
to take a look at! This is quite some fashion set of a restaurant and
someone has clearly been enjoying themselves creating it.

You'll have entered Les Rives d'Auzon via a long entrance
hall, the door to the left announcing the '*Entrée des
artistes*', in this case the way in for chefs and waiters!
This is the catwalk that Daniel Tinlot treads. A former
advertising man, he is the person who directs the
cooking here. He set up in the early 1990s. He used to
rustle up dishes for friends at weekends and so
delighted them that they suggested that he should
try to cook professionally. Now cooking has become what he
calls a *carrière de passion*. He's a very gentle man, but clearly has bold
and bright ideas. He also occasionally takes up his guitar to do his Eric
Clapton impersonation, an indication of *son look*.

As to his cuisine, he says that it's dictated by an '*esprit cuisine de
marché*'. But he also admits to trying to add a dash of
excitement to the Provençal staples. He goes to
market every day. The herbs come in the main from a
friend who grows them in a greenhouse, and he also
gets some from Georges Biscarat's L'Aromate, a
reputed specialist in Cavaillon not far away.

You're on the very edge of the old town here and it's a substantial drop
in style as well as distance down into the town ditch turned municipal

garden below, on the bank of the Auzon river. On clear days you can glimpse the Dentelles de Montmirail and the end of the Mont Ventoux in the distance.

The trouble with the material of the tablecloths is that it is provocatively sensuous. Try to keep your hands off it for a minute to consult the menus. With the *menu autour des légumes* (three courses for 130F), here is a French chef who has clearly not just heard of vegetarians, but is willing to cater for them. And there are also the superb local vegetables to make the most of. Delicious smells emerged as we cut into the *tourte aux olives de Nyons et petite salade d'ici*, an olive pie. The olive paste, made from the prized olives of Nyons, was mixed with splendid aubergines, all with a curious and delightful hint of raisins. One of the main courses on this menu was a *risotto d'épeautre aux morilles*. *Epeautre* is a kind of puffed wheat typical of the region. It has a very satisfying texture, slightly glutinous, helpful in absorbing a risotto sauce. The morel mushrooms looked like little prunes, or maybe tiny black sponges. One guest described them as tasting like mushrooms on the way to becoming truffles! A dish to linger over every mouthful.

The normal lunchtime menu comes for 85F for two courses, or 110F for three courses, but both have the added advantage of a glass of wine included. The raw salmon starter was accompanied by the strong

flavours of capers, finely chopped red onions and coloured peppercorns. The *suprême de volaille en court bouillon de citron* as a main course was given tanginess and life by the sweet onions as well as the citrus sauce.

The *menu Rives d'Auzon*, again three courses, is still a bargain at 158F. With this, you could try the *caillettes d'autrefois au parfum de sauge*, the recipe for which is given below. The choices are more exotic on this menu. The day we were there, the starters included a gazpacho of tuna and fresh salmon, a red mullet gâteau, a *compote* of sweet peppers with anchovies, and spaghetti with courgettes and chicken in a curry vinaigrette. The carpaccio of duck *magret* might come with Parmesan shavings, the young rabbit with *tapenade* and rosemary. You might also be able to choose cod or lamb, each served with garlic.

The desserts are again more varied on the more expensive menu. The *crème brûlée, sucre roux caramélisé* would match the back wall of the inner dining room rather well. The pears poached in spicy red wine came with a refreshing blackcurrant sorbet. Or you could opt for a *charlotte tiramisu* or a *fondant au chocolat* served with a cream of bitter almonds. On the *menu autour des légumes*, we also had the tempting-sounding choice of *faisselle* with honey and almonds.

Cécile is the woman who looks after you in the dining room, run off her feet most of the time. She has found the time, however, to pass a diploma as a *sommelier* or wine waiter. She chooses wines exclusively from the region. The big, classic-styled wine glasses allow you to take in the aromas fully. We tried a Domaine de Marotte 1995 white she recommended, classified merely as a *vin de pays*, but rather rich and complex, with a touch of sweetness. There is a good choice of Côtes du Ventoux, including La Croix des Pins, made by Philippe Avon at Mazan a short way east of Carpentras—he's very welcoming and might be worth visiting. The choice of Domaine de Fondrèche wines also come from Mazan and are recommended from among the range of wines listed.

Caillettes Provençales d'Autrefois

Serve this dish with a simple mixed salad dressed with olive oil.

Makes about 20 meatballs

750g/1 ½lbs lean pork
750g/1 ½lbs pork belly
1 pig's liver
1 pig's heart
1 litre/1 ¾ pints dry white wine
1 sprig rosemary, plus extra for garnishing
1 sprig sage
1.5kg/3lbs 6oz leaf spinach, fresh or frozen, defrosted
sea salt and pepper
500g/1lb 2oz pig's caul, soaked in cold water for 24 hours
1 tablespoon olive oil

Chop all the pork, including the liver and heart, into pieces about 4–5cm/1½–1¾in square. Place all the meat in a large casserole. Add the white wine, rosemary and a little of the sage. Simmer, covered, for about 1½–2 hours. Remove from the heat and leave to cool.

Preheat the oven to 110°C/225°F (gas mark ¼) and blanch the spinach in boiling water.

Remove the pieces of meat from the casserole and mince together with the spinach in a food processor. Chop the remaining fresh sage finely and add it to the mixture. Form it into small, even-shaped meatballs, wrapping them in squares of the pig's caul. Place in an ovenproof dish and cook for 40 minutes in the preheated oven.

Serve warm. Dress with a little sea salt and pepper and drizzle the olive oil over the meatballs. Garnish with the remaining sprigs of rosemary.

---

touring around

Before lunch, penetrate into the centre of **Carpentras** via the towering Porte d'Orange, built in the 1360s under Pope Innocent IV. The average French town of 30,000 or so, unless it has some great historical importance or major monument, is likely to be a rather anonymous place. Carpentras isn't. Perhaps because of its long isolation from the rest of France, under papal rule but really run by its own bishops, the city has character and a subtle but distinct sense of place. A bit unkempt, and unconcerned about it, immune to progress and to any sudden urges for urban renewal, it is nevertheless an interesting town to visit. There are some cockeyed monuments, and some surprises. The rest of Provence pays Carpentras little mind; ask anyone, and they'll probably remember only that the town is famous for caramels, mint-flavoured ones called *berlingots*. The gorgeous produce of the Comtat Venaissin farmers rolls in for Friday market. The stands fill half the town, but the centre is Rue des Halles, with the Passage Boyer, an imposing glass-roofed arcade, built by Carpentras' unemployed in the national public works programme started after the 1848 revolution.

The **Cathédrale St-Siffrein** is undoubtedly one of the most absurd cathedrals in Christendom. So many architects, in so many periods, and no one has ever been able to get it finished and get it right. Worst of all is the mongrel façade—Baroque on the bottom, a bit of Gothic and who knows what else above. Begun in the 1400s, remodellings and restorations proceeded in fits and starts until 1902. Some of the original intentions can be seen in the fine Flamboyant Gothic portal on the southern side, called the Porte Juive because Jewish converts were taken through it, in suitably humiliating ceremonies for the Christians, to be baptized. Just above the centre of the arch is Carpentras's famous curio, the small sculpted *Boule aux Rats*—a globe covered with rats. The usual explanation is that this has something to do with the Jews, or heretics. But bigotry was never really fashionable among 15th-century artists, and more likely this is a joke on an old fanciful etymology of the town's name: *carpet ras*, or 'the rat nibbles'.

The interior, richly decorated in dubious taste, includes some stained glass of the 1500s (much restored) and an early 15th-century altar-piece (left of the high altar) by Enguerrand Quarton of the Avignon school. The sacred treasures are in a chapel on the left: the relics of St Siffrein, one of the most obscure of all saints, not even mentioned in any early hagiographies; and the Saint-Mors, the 'holy bridle bit', said to have been made by St Helen out of two nails of Christ's Cross as a present for her son, Emperor Constantine.

Next to the cathedral, the **Palais de Justice** (1640) is the former Archbishop's Palace, occupying the site of an earlier palace that, for the brief periods that popes like Innocent IV chose to stay in Carpentras, was the centre of the Christian world. The present building, modelled after the Farnese Palace in Rome, contains some frescoes from the 17th and 18th centuries worth casting an eye over, showing mythological scenes, and also views of Comtat Venaissin villages and towns (ask the concierge to be shown round).

Everyone knows that if you walk around a church widdershins (against the sun: counter-clockwise), you'll end up in fairyland, like Childe Harolde. Try it in Carpentras, and you'll find some strange business. The 9m Roman **Triumphal Arch**, tucked in a corner between the Cathedral and the Palais de Justice, was built about the same time as that of Orange, in the early 1st century AD. Anyone who hasn't yet seen Orange's would hardly guess this one was Roman at all. Of all the ancient Provençal monuments, this shows the bizarre Celtic quality of Gallo-Roman art at its most stylized extreme, with its reliefs of enchained captives and trophies. In the 1300s, the arch was incorporated into the now-lost Episcopal Palace. By 1640, when it was cleared, it was serving an inglorious role separating the archbishop's kitchens from his prisons. Originally, it must have connected the palace with the Romanesque cathedral.

Now, look at the clumsily built exterior wall of the present cathedral, opposite the arch. There are two large gaps, through which you can have a peek at something that few books mention, and that even the Carpentrassiens themselves seem to have forgotten: the crossing and cupola of the 12th-century cathedral, used in the rebuilt church to support a bell tower (later demolished) and neglected for centuries. In its time this must have been one of the greatest buildings of Provence, done in an ambitious, classicizing style—perhaps too ambitious, since its partial collapse in 1399 necessitated the rebuilding. The sculpted decoration, vine and acanthus-leaf patterns, along with winged creatures and scriptural scenes, is excellent work; some of it has been moved to the town museum.

In the afternoon, make for the extraordinary spring of Fontaine-de-Vaucluse, south from Carpentras, stopping on your way at Pernes-les-Fontaines or L'Isle-sur-la-Sorgue. **Pernes-les-Fontaines** has only the single drowsy stream of the Nesque passing through it. In the 18th century, perhaps out of jealousy towards L'Isle sur-la-Sorgue, the Pernois took it into their heads to build decorative fountains instead. They got a bit carried away, and now there are 37 of them, or one for every 200 or so inhabitants. The fountains contribute a lot to making Pernes one of the most delightful towns in the Vaucluse.

The Sorgue, that singular river that jumps out of the ground at Fontaine-de-Vaucluse and is one of France's best trout streams, briefly splits into two channels at **L'Isle-sur-la-Sorgue** to make this Provençal 'Venice', a charming town of 17,000 souls, an island indeed. In the Middle Ages, as a scrappy semi-independent *commune*, L'Isle-sur-la-Sorgue dug two more channels, and put the water to work running mills and textile factories. Today, L'Isle-sur-la-Sorgue is best known as the antiques centre of Provence, with a number of permanent shops on the southern edge of town, around Avenue des Quatre Otages, and a big 'Antiques Village' by the train station, open on Sundays (some booths open Sat and Mon also).

East of L'Isle-sur-la-Sorgue you'll find **Fontaine-de-Vaucluse**. Over a century ago, explorers found the source of the Nile. They're still looking for the source of the little Vaucluse river of the Sorgue. It's underground; the best spelunkers in France have been combing the region's caves for decades, and in the eighties three submarine probes were sent down to investigate, none of them with much success.

The Fontaine is still an exquisite place, but the 540 or so residents of the village of Fontaine-de-Vaucluse have not been able to keep the place from being transformed into one of Provence's more garish tourist traps. To reach it, from the car park next to the church, you'll have to walk a noisy 2km gauntlet of commerciality, everything from *frites* stands to a museum of authentic Provençal *santons*, and a museum of medieval torture instruments along the way. Incredibly, several of the attractions are worthwhile. There is Norbert Castaret's **Subterranean World**, a museum of underground rarities and informational exhibits overseen by France's best-known cave explorer (*open 10–12 and 2–6; closed Tues, Jan and Feb*) and **Vallis Clausa**, a paper-mill powered by old wooden wheels in the river that keeps up an old craft tradition on the Sorgue, making paper the 15th-century way for art books and stationery (*open 10–8, closed Tues: guided tours and sales*).

Finally, there is the **source** itself, well worth the trouble even in its off-season. In the spring, and occasionally in winter, it pours out at a rate of as much as 200 cubic metres per second, forming a small, intensely green lake under the cliff. From the late spring until autumn it is greatly diminished, and often stops overflowing altogether (the water appears slightly further down the cliff); its unpredictability is as much a mystery as its source. You can climb up to the romantically ruined 13th-century château overlooking the spring.

Papal Pleasures in Avignon

the bridge of Avignon & walls of the Papal Palace

Avignon is pure theatre, and you can certainly feel in the midst of the action when you're here. Even outside the July madness of the Festival d'Avignon, the city bustles with life. The main set provided by history is preposterously good, an old city by the Rhône surrounded by a vast crenellated wall. Within, you can wander through a variety of backdrops—plane-shaded café-lined streets, religious quarters turned into smart residential areas, last-century boulevards and the giant stage of the Place du Palais des Papes, one of France's truly great squares.

The story line is pretty mean too. A French pope, Clement V, fleeing the urban upheaval of early 14th-century Rome, plumped for a patch in Provence that the papacy had won for its persecuting part in the then recent Albigensian Crusades. Clement V and his successors settled into a lavish life style and each played his part in developing an ever-growing Gothic monster of a palace as the city fell prey to outrageous decadence. The seventh Avignon pope, Gregory XI, went back to Rome in 1377 for a brief look to see if conditions there had improved and, before he had time to run back to Provence, died. The Italians seized upon the opportunity to grab their papacy back. But the French went and elected their own choice, giving birth to the Great Schism. The confusion was settled at the start of the 15th century, Rome regaining its undisputed position as seat of the papacy. But cardinal-legates ruled Avignon and their Comtat Venaissin territories in Provence in no mean style for centuries to come.

There are entertaining side stories too, like that broken bridge on which the song says people once danced so manically, and the papal vineyards. The great vinegrowing gravels of Châteauneuf-du-Pape lie up the Rhône valley and provided the setting for papal summer parties. Closer to modern times, in the 19th century, Avignon itself, with its long tradition of publishing, became the centre of production for the Félibrige, a group of literary figures fighting to protect Provençal culture.

Today, back on the square in front of the Palais des Papes, you may well find buskers vying ruthlessly for attention. The tourists gawp. It's hard not to when standing below the intimidating, lance-arched Gothic façade of the palace of the papal 'Babylonian exile', as Petrarch termed the papacy's stay here. We'd strongly suggest you sit down for an *apéritif* in this square to steel yourselves before plunging into the debauched back-alleys of Avignon to find L'Epicerie, not some spicy grocer's store, but a highly seductive restaurant.

getting there

The easiest place to park for this central location in Avignon is in the underground car park under the Place du Palais, the heart of Avignon. From here to the Place St-Pierre you go from the greatest square in Avignon (arguably one of the greatest in the whole of

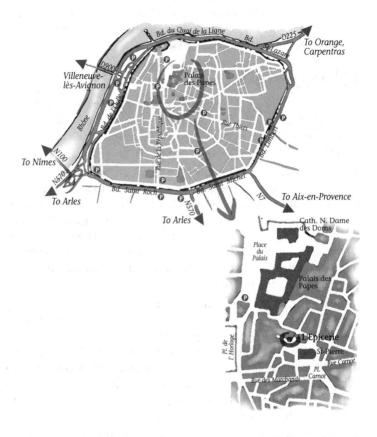

France) to one of the most intimate and picturesque in the city (and, yes, arguably in France). Take the alley down the right-hand side of the palace, passing under a vast supporting flying buttress and by large chunks of rock which demonstrate how the popes took the parable literally and built their home on solid rock. You come out in front of the satyr-fronted Hôtel La Mirande. Resist the temptation of its splendid 17th-century entrance (you can try its restaurant another time) and take the street to the right of it, the Rue Peyrolerie, past a plaque commemorating a terrible recent murder that took place here. The Rue Peyrolerie leads into a quarter of chic houses, little religious statues gracing street corners. The Place St-Pierre lies discreetly just down to the right of the first streets off the Rue Peyrolerie.

L'Epicerie

Restaurant L'Epicerie, 10 Place St-Pierre, 84000 Avignon, ☎ 04 90 82 74 22. Closed Sat lunchtime and Sun all day; in June, closed Sun lunchtime only; annual closure end Nov–early April. Reasonable value à la carte options. French songs Sat evening once a month.

You have to trust in God or the gods that it doesn't rain if you book lunch at L'Epicerie. For the greatest pleasure of arriving at the restaurant is to realize that you're going to eat outside, in the presence of one of the best companions that Christianity can offer to non-believer and believer alike, a beautiful, edifying church. The church of St-Pierre isn't so much like a guest at another table; rather, given its imposing proximity, it's more like a parental figure watching over everything the little children eat.

It's reassuring, with this church staring so paternally down at you, that L'Epicerie is an unassuming kind of place, without pretentions or airs. The tablecloths are in that popular French chequered style, in plastic. The salt and pepper shakers are exactly the kind you'd buy from the grocer's for your basic home cooking. The array of ordinary tables and chairs which spread out from the small, single narrow café room onto the cobbled square is slightly protected from the general public's gaze by a row of generous-leaved plants.

The restaurant façade, with fairy lights strung under the awning, has faded green shutters leading up to an Italian-style open upper gallery. A trip up the treacherous wooden winding staircase to the loo on the first floor affords you a good glimpse into the kitchen. It isn't soigné, but it is characterful. Take the time, before descending, to enjoy the view down from here onto the diners below and the different perspective on the church façade.

Before turning to the menu, a description of the little café-turned-restaurant room. This is painted a dried blood red, but is womb-cosy rather than threatening. With a long banquette running along one side, there's not much room for more than a handful of tables. Odd old tins, posters and Dubonnet signs decorate the inside, recalling an old grocer's store. And there's a large painting of a Breton port scene, which gives away the origins of one of the principal young women to run the place, Florence Oliver. Casually trendy in a cool but welcoming way, she helps prepare the cuisine at lunchtime while her partners organize it in the evening.

There is no set menu at L'Epicerie, but three courses will come to around 140F. For a smaller but very satisfying meal you could try one of the copious *assiettes* and then have cheese or a pudding, which would set you back around 100F, as would a two-course meal. The choice is good, but the best thing about the cooking here is the expert dosage of fine, fresh ingredients. The flavours aren't overdone, and the general experience is of satisfying food, the tastes gentle and pleasing.

The starter of *compote glacée de courgettes*, for example, was so delicately flavoured with aniseed that anyone who has been put off in the past by aniseed's strong flavour should be converted. With the nice, slightly coarse consistency of the *compote*, the flavour of courgettes, that can be rather meek, was well pepped up by the aniseed and by basil. The *assiette provençale* would be an excellent choice of starter if you're hungry. It gives you the chance to try a whole range of the house specialities as so many little tasters. The *courgette compote* is included; so are *aubergines confites*, of deepest papal-purple skin, preserved in olive oil; a thin, beaten slice of *tarte à la tomate et au basilic*; a piece of hot St-Marcellin cheese on toast, a portion of the red mullet main course; salad, melon, *jambon cru*...enough to make you feel extremely satisfied. Moving to the *assiette des Epicières*, this is centred round tuna, grilled wild leeks, a *tartine* of *tapenade*, French beans, tomatoes, chickpeas, radish, celeriac, anchovies...all covered with olive oil. *Cébettes*, we discovered, is a name for new onions. Among other appealing starters, you could try peppers stuffed with cod and spices or *terrine de foie de volaille* served with *oignons confits* and a salad.

The presentation of the dishes shows touches of humour. For the main course, the red mullet and potatoes in the delicious *filets de rougets à la fondue de poivrons et coriandre fraîche* was made to look temptingly confusing, like pieces of figs alternating with slices of pale melon. For a local meat speciality, try the *boeuf des mariniers du Rhône*. A passing acknowledgement is made to that other papal city with the *saltimbocca à la romaine*, served with aubergine fritters, while some homage is paid to Brittany in the use of reputed Guérande salt and Breton butter. The sauté of lamb may come with almonds and aubergines, the leg of lamb with mild garlic cream and *ratatouille*, the *magret* of duck with an aniseed-flavoured purée and tomatoes gratinéd with parmesan and orange. So many exotic touches, expertly done.

The choice of Côtes-du-Rhône or Rhône estuary Grand Delta wines are served in generous glasses. It would seem only appropriate to try a Châteauneuf-du-Pape. An inspiration to both popes and lovers, Châteauneuf-du-Pape's reputation has remained strong through the ages; to safeguard it in 1923 its growers agreed to the guarantees and controls that formed the basis for France's modern *appellation d'origine contrôlée* laws. Several factors combine to give the wine its unique character: the alluvial red clay and pebbly soil, brought down by a Rhône glacier in the ice age; the *mistral* which chases away the clouds and haze, letting the sun hit the grapes like an X-ray gun; and the wide palette of grape varieties that each winemaker can choose from.

The puddings leave a delicious taste in the mouth. The *pêches blanches au jus de groseille et glace à la vanille* combined the freshest of peaches with sweet vanilla ice cream, offset by the tanginess of a redcurrant sauce. There are puddings for the more mature palate as well, such as the cream of mascarpone with coffee and whisky, or the popular *faisselle artisanale au marc de Provence*, the fromage blanc scattered with raisins well doused in Provençal *eau de vie*, a delicious *digestif* of a dessert.

Compote Glacée de Courgettes

Serves 6

6 courgettes, chopped
1 litre/1 ¾ pints chicken stock
2 green peppers
2 tomatoes
2 garlic cloves
1 onion
2 tablespoons olive oil
2 limes
1 teaspoon fennel seeds
1 tablespoon chopped fresh basil leaves
salt and pepper
3 pieces sliced bread, fried, to serve

Steam the courgettes together with ½ a lime for 10 minutes, then transfer to a food processor, discarding the lime. Cut a shallow cross into the top of each tomato and blanch for about 30 seconds, then plunge into cold water. The skins will loosen. Peel them off and dice finely. To peel the peppers, either grill them or stick a fork into the stem end and hold them over a high gas flame until the skin blackens and turn until charred all over. Plunge them into cold water and then rub off the skins. Chop the flesh.

Peel and chop the garlic and the onion. Add them, half the tomato and two-thirds of the peppers to the steamed courgettes, together with the basil, olive oil, juice from the remaining ½ lime, the stock, and salt and pepper to taste. Process until smooth, then pour the mixture into a plastic container and put it into the freezer to chill.

Remove and garnish with the remaining chopped tomato and green pepper and the fennel seeds. Serve with the pieces of fried bread and the second lime cut into 6 wedges.

touring around

After lunch, you'll be irresistibly drawn to take a closer look at Avignon's **church of St-Pierre** and the cobbled streets around the square. A dark alley leads off from one corner. A secretive museum hides in another, Avignon's cosiest, the **Musée Aubanel** (*private, free visits on request, © 04 90 82 95 54*), dedicated to printing in Avignon, and to the Romantic poet and Félibre Théodore Aubanel, whose family still owns one of Avignon's oldest publishing houses. You could delve further into the streets and squares around St-Pierre with their religious, residential and shopping delights.

Devote your morning to the Place du Palais. When the Church had picked up the Comtat Venaissin piece of Provence real estate as its spoils after the Albigensian Crusade, isolated within it was the little city-republic of Avignon, belonging to the Angevin counts of Provence—old papal allies, who welcomed their illustrious visitor. Clement V always intended to return to Rome, but when he died the French cardinals elected a former archbishop of Avignon John XXII (1316–34), who moved the Curia into his old episcopal palace and greatly enriched the papacy (through alchemy, it was rumoured). Although he enlarged the palace with the proceeds, it still wasn't roomy enough for his successor, Benedict XII (1334–42), who replaced it with another palace, or for Clement VI (1342–52), who added another.

'You would think it was an Asiatic tyrant's citadel rather than the abode of the vicar of the God of peace', wrote Mérimée of the **Palais des Papes** (*open daily April–Oct 9–7, till 8 in Sept; Nov–Mar 9–12.45 and 2–6; adm. Last ticket 45 mins before closing time. Optional guided tours in English at 3pm*). After crossing the Cour d'Honneur, the great court-yard dividing Benedict XII's stern Cistercian Palais Vieux (1334–42) from Clement VI's flamboyant Palais Neuf (1342–52), the tour begins in the Jesus Hall, so called for its decorative monograms of Christ. Once used to house the pope's treasure and account books, it now contains a hoard of maps, views of old Avignon and curios like a pair of 17th-century bell-ringing figures, or *Jacquemarts*. The most valuable loot would be stored behind walls 3m thick in the windowless bowels of the Angels' Tower, its ceiling supported by a single stone pillar like an enormous palm tree.

Next, the Consistory, where the cardinals met and received ambassadors; as its lavish frescoes and ceiling burned in 1413, it now displays 19th-century portraits of Avignon's popes and Simone Martini's fresco of the *Virgin of Humility*, detached from the cathedral porch in 1960. Traces of walls prepared for painting are to be seen in the Chapelle St-Jean, dedicated to both Johns, the Baptist and the Evangelist. Matteo Giovannetti of Viterbo, a *trecento* charmer who left the bulk of his work in Avignon, did the frescoes for Clement VI; saints float overhead in starry blue landscapes (recall that at the time ultramarine blue paint was even more expensive than gold). On one wall, John's head is blissfully served to Herod at table, as if in a restaurant.

The tour continues to the first floor and the banqueting hall, or Grand Tinel, hung with 18th-century Gobelin tapestries. Although big enough for a football pitch, the Grand Tinel was too small to hold all the cardinal-electors who would gather in a conclave ten days after a pope's death. Masons were brought in to accommodate them: the arches on the far end were knocked down to give the cardinals more room to manoeuvre, while the doors and windows were bricked up to keep them from bringing in more food and endlessly prolonging the conclave. The trick always worked, for the appetites of the 14th-century Curia were Gargantuan—the adjacent Upper Kitchen boasts a pyramidal chimney that could easily handle a roast elephant, or the menu of Clement VI's coronation feast: 1023 sheep, 118 cattle, 101 calves, 914 kids, 60 pigs, 10,471 hens, 1446 geese, 300 pike, topped off by 46,856 cheeses and 50,000 tarts, all consumed by just 3000 guests. Off the Grand Tinel, more delightful frescoes by Matteo Giovannetti decorate the Chapelle St-Martial, celebrating the French saint who came from the same Limousin village as Benedict XII.

The tour takes you on to the pope's antechamber, where he would hold private audiences, and continues to the Pope's bedroom in the Tower of Angels, a room covered with enchanting murals of spiralling foliage, birds, and birdcages. It leads directly into the New Palace and the most delightful room in the entire place, the Chambre du Cerf,

Clement VI's study, where he would come 'to seek the freedom of forgetting he was pope'. In 1343 he had Matteo Giovannetti (probably) lead a group of French painters in depicting outdoor scenes of hunting, fishing, and peach-picking that not only quickened the papal gastric juices, but expressed what was then a revolutionary new interest in the natural world, where flowers and foliage were drawn from observation rather than copying a 'source'.

The arrows direct you next to the Sacristy, crowded with statues of kings, queens, and bishops escaped from Gargantua's chessboard, followed by Clement VI's Great Chapel, longer even than the Grand Tinel and just as empty, although the altar has recently been reconstructed. The Robing Room off the chapel contains casts of the Avignon popes' tombs. Revolutionaries bashed most of the figures that once adorned the elaborate chapel gate; through the bay window in front of this, the pope would bless and give indulgences to pilgrims. A grand stair leads down to the Flamboyant Great Audience Hall, where a band of Matteo Giovannetti's *Prophets* remain intact, along with outline sketches of a *Crucifixion* that would have been splendid if it had ever been completed.

To the left of the palace is Avignon's cathedral, **Notre-Dame-des-Doms**, built in 1150, its landmark square bell tower ridiculously dwarfed by a massive gilt statue of the Virgin added in 1859, an unsuccessful attempt to make the church stand out next to the overwhelming papal pile. The interior has been fuzzily Baroqued, looking the architectural equivalent of a soft-centre chocolate, but it's worth focusing on the good bits: the dome at the crossing, with an octagonal drum pierced with light, the masterpiece of this typically Provençal conceit; the 11th- or 12th-century marble bishop's chair in the choir; and in a chapel next to the sacristy, the flamboyant Tomb of John XXII (d. 1334) by English sculptor Hugh Wilfred, mutilated in the Revolution, and restored in the 19th century with a spare effigy of a bishop on top to replace the smashed pope.

Overlooking the Rhône at the end of the Place des Papes stands the **Petit Palais**. Reserve this visit for the afternoon (*open 9.30–11.50 and 2–6, closed Tues; adm*). The palace was built in 1318 and modified in 1474 to suit the tastes of Cardinal Legate Giuliano della Rovere—one day to become Michelangelo's patron and nemesis, as Pope Julius II. In 1958, the Petit Palais became a museum to hold all the medieval works remaining in Avignon. Although the scale of the Petit Palais can be daunting, it contains rare treats from the dawn of the Renaissance by artists hailing for the most part from Siena or Florence. But Avignon gets its say as well: the sculptures, pretty courtly frescoes and paintings from the 12th to the 15th century demonstrate the city's role in creating and diffusing the late International Gothic style. But the museum's best-known work is Botticelli's *Virgin and Child*, a tender, lyrical painting from his youth, inspired by his master, Verrochio.

Below the walls of the papal quarter, four arches of a bridge leapfrog into the Rhône, sidle up to a waterbound Romanesque chapel (dedicated to St Nicholas, the patron of sailors), and then stop abruptly mid-river, long before reaching Villeneuve-lès-Avignon on the distant bank. This is the famous **Pont St-Bénézet**, or simply the Pont d'Avignon, begun in 1185 (*open daily Easter–Sept 9–6.30, Oct–Easter 9–1 and 2–5, closed Mon*). It was built at a time when all bridges were the work of either devils or saints; in this case a shepherd boy named Bénézet, obeying the mandates of heaven, single-handedly laid the huge foundation stones. Originally 22 arches and half a mile long, the bridge enriched Avignon with its tolls: its presence was a major factor in the popes' decision to live here. In 1660 the Avignonais got tired of the constant repairs it demanded, however, and abandoned it to the Rhône.

And did they ever '*danse, tout en rond*' on their bridge, as the nursery song would have it? No, the historians say, although they may well have danced under it on the mid-river Ile de la Barthelasse, formerly a hunting reserve and headquarters for many of Avignon's prostitutes and thieves. It was here that in later years the Avignonais came for Sunday picnics. In the summer, people still come for entertainment, in its Olympic-size pool.

After all that sightseeing, you might consider devoting another day to discovering the papal vineyards of Chateauneuf-du-Pape, some 20km north of Provence's papal seat.

Van Gogh's Tormented Alpilles

The viciously sharp teeth of the little mountain chain of Les Alpilles jut out of the land a short distance south of Avignon. From the papal city to these jagged pinnacles, the road takes you past bowed bamboo hedges and curtains of deeply dark cypresses, their scraggy tops the type Van Gogh cooked into a boiling, seething mass when he was in such a mental stew. The maddening *mistral* plays havoc here, and the farmers have divided their plots into thin wind-shielded strips to protect the fertile earth.

To appreciate the lie of the land, you could make a swift detour into Châteaurenard and climb to the hilltop castle to take in the views south. On the flat land just to the north of the Alpilles sits the old village of St-Rémy-de-Provence. It protects itself behind a reassuringly thick ring of plane trees so typical of Provence and immortalized by Van Gogh. Many a famous name is linked with St-Rémy apart from the Dutch painter who spent his terrifying final year of life in the asylum here.

L'Assiette de Marie

Nostradamus was born here. Gertrude Stein spent years in the village. And in the First World War, when interned Germans were apportioned rooms in the asylum, Albert Schweitzer was allocated Van Gogh's former cell. St-Rémy has since been more prosaically 'discovered' by wealthy Parisians and a plethora of other visitors.

A short ride or a good walk south out of town takes you to the ruins of a Roman city named Glanum, and two completely intact ancient funeral monuments called Les Antiques.

Heading south from St-Rémy, the road winds up into the deserted, scrubby, barren hills of the Alpilles. Now one of the most famous tourist villages in France, in medieval times Les Baux was the hide-out of one of the most successfully rebellious and anarchistic lines of counts of southern France. There's little secrecy to the village today. Although the buildings still merge surreptitiously with the rock, in summer mile upon mile of cars parked along the road give away its location.

St-Rémy is not exactly cheap, but there are some unpretentious good restaurants here and, although Princess Caroline and the rest of the royal family of Monaco have apparently been known to pop in occasionally to our restaurant for the day (the Grimaldi family used to own St-Rémy), L'Assiette de Marie is a relaxed and charming place to eat.

getting there

St-Rémy-de-Provence lies some 20 km due south of Avignon. A ring of plane trees surrounds the centre of the old town. Try either parking in their shade, or head for the large car park by the tourist office a very short way outside the centre. Then walk into the small heart of the town. The Rue Jaume Roux connects the Place Pelissier with the Place Joseph Hilaire. The restaurant is just a little north of this last, almost opposite the Passage Blain.

L'Assiette de Marie

L'Assiette de Marie, 1 Rue Jaume Roux, 13210 St-Rémy-de-Provence, © 04 90 92 32 14. Open Easter–Sept lunchtimes and evenings; rest of year open evenings and only Wed and weekend lunchtimes. Menu at 135F on weekday lunchtimes, otherwise at 169F.

Marie is the young woman in her early twenties who has created the ambiance and manages the cooking here. While she's in the kitchen, Max, a loud and jovial spirit, greets you warmly, even if he sometimes

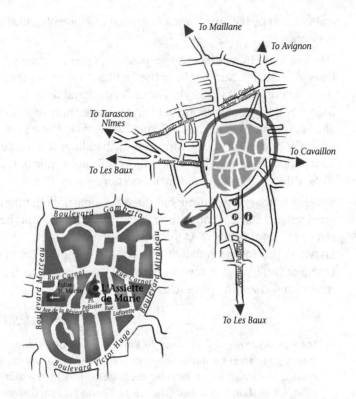

To Maillane

To Avignon

To Tarascon
Nîmes

To Cavaillon

To Les Baux

Avenue Gabriel & René Taillandier

Avenue Louis Mistral

Avenue Fouconuts

Avenue Pasteur

Boulevard Gambetta

Boulevard Marceau

Rue Carnot

Rue Carnot

Boulevard Mirabeau

Église
St. Martin

L'Assiette
de Marie

Pl.
Pelissier

Rue
Lafayette

Ave. de la Résistance

Boulevard Victor Hugo

To Les Baux

lays it on a bit thick. But it's nice because it's so evident that he wants to please. Show songs backed his banter when we went along.

With its intimate rooms packed with so many bits and pieces, the place incites you to conversation. One of the two front rooms into which you can peer from the street actually looks remarkably like an old granny's sitting room, full of mementoes and family pieces. And indeed that's pretty much what it turns out to be; Marie bought the old lady's house next door to help enlarge her original premises, knocked a low door in the wall, and decked out what had been the old lady's front room. Lampshades in cloth, old pots, clocks and photos, small furniture, an outmoded air cooler and gramophone, unframed pictures on the wall... The décor is a bit contrived, but the cultivated old-fashioned feel works. Several passers-by greet Max through the open window while he is serving, stopping for a quick chat. The room by which you enter the restaurant, also a dining room, is slightly darker and cosier. The third dining room has a more theatrical, backstage feel, with mirrors bordered by hats, a bar, and an unmissable coquettish naked woman, proudly displaying her prominent naked backside, one foot on a *boules* ball. The tradition in these parts, so we were told, is for the loser of a game of *boules* to be forced to kiss Fanny's bottom.

The menu, scrawled on blackboards, is simple and makes the most of Provence's vegetable delights. The day we were there, the choice of starters was between warmed Alpilles goat's cheese on a bed of mixed salads, preserved red peppers grilled in olive oil, a *panaché* of tomatoes, mozzarella and *pistounade*, or *l'assiette de Marie*. This last really outshines the others, not surprisingly, as it includes a taster of most of them, as well as little artichokes or asparagus, *tapenade*, chickpeas, and a caviar of aubergines divine enough to make a Turkish *imam* faint.

The vegetable theme continues into the main courses, with an excellent lasagne cooked with ten different types of vegetables, much garlic accompanying the aubergines, courgettes, carrots, shallots, celeriac...you'll have to work out the rest. All extremely tasty, but we couldn't help feeling surprised when we heard a woman who'd arrived at the next table ask which dishes didn't contain any garlic. Our witty waiter couldn't help smiling and explained that only with the puddings was it really possible to avoid the stuff. He said he would ask the cook if she could remove some. A harsher man might have questioned what the poor woman was doing at all in a Provence restaurant if she couldn't abide the blessed alliaceous bulb.

The cannelloni filling combines *brousse de brebis*, a ewe's milk cheese, with fresh spinach. Moving to the meat, you could choose between lamb stew or farm-reared rabbit, in typical Provençal sauces. These dishes aren't out of the ordinary in the region, but they are very satisfying. Some of the wines at L'Assiette de Marie are more exclusive. The Château Romanin is produced just east of St-Rémy (south off the D99) by the patron of Les Baux's famous restaurant, the Oustau de Baumanière. The Domaine de Trévallon lies next door to it. These count among some of the most complex wines in Provence. Max can also advise you on slightly more modest bottles and tell you how to visit the vineyards. For a surprise on the menu, look out for the *suggestion de Marie au retour du marché*, which depends on what she's found in the market.

Don't expect matching china at L'Assiette de Marie, but instead an eccentric mix of plates. The fruit salad of three peaches came in a charmingly chipped banana-shaped dish. The three types of peach are the most scented and sweet white peach, the more common yellow peach, and the *pêche de vigne*, the vineyard peach, a very large variety, very red on the outside, white within. Another simple and satisfying pudding is the strawberries in a sweet sugar sauce. Otherwise, there are the old classics, *crème brûlée*, *fondant au chocolat*, *nougat glacé* and *île flottante*.

Cannelloni à la Brousse de Brebis

Serves 6

1kg/2lbs 4oz fresh spinach

4 tablespoons olive oil

salt and pepper

50g/2oz butter

1kg/2lbs 4oz ewe's milk cheese

250g/9oz Gruyère cheese, grated

2 fresh eggs

5 onions, finely chopped

8 shallots, finely chopped

2 tablespoons chopped fresh parsley

2 garlic cloves, crushed

2kg/4 ½lbs fresh tomatoes, skinned, deseeded and chopped

1 tablespoon chopped fresh thyme

pinch of sugar

500g/1lb 2oz fresh lasagne sheets

250ml/8fl oz crème fraîche

olive oil

*Wash the spinach thoroughly, drain well and remove the stalks. Sauté
gently in half the olive oil until the spinach has wilted. Season with salt and
pepper. Add the butter. Let it melt, stir well, then take the pan off the heat.*

*Put the ewe's milk cheese, grated cheese (reserving a good handful), eggs
and then the spinach into a large bowl. Mix well until smooth.*

*Sauté the chopped onions and shallots in the remaining oil until they turn
golden, then add the parsley and garlic. Take half of the onion
mixture and blend it well into the* brousse de brebis *and
spinach mixture. Add the other half to the tomatoes, season
with salt and pepper and thyme, and add the pinch of
sugar to cut the acidity of the tomatoes. Cook for 10 minutes.*

*Preheat the oven to 180°C/350°F (gas mark 4). Meanwhile, cut the pasta
into strips approximately 10cm/4in wide, place a strip of stuffing about
2.5cm/1in wide along each strip and roll the stuffing in the pasta. Place in
an ovenproof dish, seam-side down, and pour the tomato sauce over the
cannelloni. Dot the crème fraîche over the top and sprinkle the reserved
grated cheese over. Bake in the preheated oven for about 20 minutes.*

---

touring around

Go to **Les Baux** early, before the crowds. Van Gogh and cypresses,
lushness and flowers are left behind with St-Rémy; in a matter of minutes the road has brought you to another world. This world of the
Alpilles is at most 16km across, and a stone's throw from the swamps
of the Camargue and the sea. It is made of thin, cool breezes and brilliant light; its colours are white and deep green—almost exclusively—
in an astringent landscape of limestone crags and patches of *maquis*,
Mediterranean scrubland.

From as early as 3000 BC, this exotic *massif* attracted residents. The
Alpilles are full of caves, many of which were once inhabited. The
Ligurians took advantage of its natural defences to found an important *oppidum* at Les Baux, the steep barren plateau in the centre of the
massif. In the Middle Ages, this made the perfect setting for the most
feared and celebrated of Provence's noble clans. The Seigneurs des
Baux are first heard of in the 900s. They never acknowledged the

authority of the French king, the Holy Roman Emperors, or just about anyone else, and their impregnable crag in the Alpilles allowed them to get away with it.

For the next two centuries the lords of Baux waged incessant warfare on all comers, and occasionally on each other, gradually becoming a real power in Provence. The family headquarters at Les Baux maintained a polished court where troubadours were always welcome. It ended with a bang in 1372, when an even nastier fellow took over the clan: Raymond de Turenne, a distant relation who was also a nephew of Pope Gregory IX. Taking advantage of confused times, in the reign of Queen Jeanne, this ambitious and bloodthirsty intriguer found enough support, and enough foreign mercenaries, to bring full-scale civil war to Provence, causing the same kind of misery to which the rest of France had become accustomed in the Hundred Years War.

When the last heir of Les Baux died in 1426, the possessions of the house were incorporated into the County of Provence. That isn't quite the end of the story; in the 1500s Les Baux began to thrive once more, first under Anne of Montmorency (a man, and one of the great political figures in 16th-century France), who rebuilt the *seigneurs'* castle in the best Renaissance taste, and later under the Manvilles, who inherited it and made it a Protestant stronghold in the Wars of Religion. Cardinal Richelieu finally put this trouble spot to rest in 1632, demolishing the castle and sending the owners the bill for the job. Until the Revolution, the remains of Les Baux were, like St-Rémy, in the hands of the Grimaldis of Monaco.

In the last 50 years, Les Baux has become the second-biggest provincial tourist attraction in France after the Mont St-Michel. The village below the castle has been rebuilt and repopulated in the worst way, and whatever spark of glamour survives in this tremendous ruin, if you come here during the day you will have to run the gauntlet of shops peddling trinkets, knick-knackery, scowling dolls, herbs, *santons* and soaps to reach it.

The first sight to greet you as you trudge up to the village is an elegant carved Renaissance fireplace, open to the sky and standing next to a souvenir shop. Further up, past the ramparts, is the Porte d'Eyguères, until the 18th century the only entrance to the city. Up the Rue de la

Calade you will come to the **Place de l'Eglise**, where the 16th-century Hôtel des Porcelets has now become the Musée Yves Brayer. Brayer's major works are here; pictures of Spain and Italy as well as Provence. Even if 20th-century figurative art isn't quite your thing, peek into the 17th-century **Chapelle des Pénitents Blancs** opposite, to see what he made of its interior (*open April–Sept 10–12 and 2–6.30, Oct–Mar 10–12 and 2–5, closed Jan–mid-Feb*). Lastly on the Place de l'Eglise stands the Eglise St-Vincent, dating from the 12th and 16th centuries. There's a Cistercian nave and 20th-century stained glass by Ingrand to peer at.

When you see the **Citadel** (*adm*) itself the ambiance changes abruptly —to a rocky chaos surrealistically decorated with fragments of once-imposing buildings. The path leads through this 'Ville Morte' to the tip of the plateau, where there is a monument to a Provençal poet Charlon Rieu, and a grand view over the Alpilles.

Turning back, the path climbs up to the château itself, with bits of towers and walls everywhere, including the apse of a Gothic chapel cut out of the rock, and the long eastern wall that survived Richelieu's explosives, dotted with finely carved windows. What looks like a monolithic honeycomb is really a 13th-century dovecot. Recent excavations have uncovered medieval tombs and foundations. The only intact part is the donjon, a rather treacherous climb to the top for a bird's-eye view over the site. Locals say the best time to see it is with a blanket, under a starry night.

Beneath Les Baux lies the **Val d'Enfer**, the wildest corner of the Alpilles, a weird landscape of eroded limestone, caves and quarries. One thing the Alpilles has a lot of is aluminium ore—*bauxite*, named after Les Baux, a useless mineral until the process for smelting it was discovered in the last century. Today the quarries host one of Les Baux's big attractions: the **Cathédrale des Images**, a slick show where 30 projectors bounce giant pictures over the walls.

The **Coteaux des Baux-en-Provence**, the AOC wine of the Alpilles, produce much rosé, like several of Provence's wine-producing areas, but in recent years the reds of Les Baux have made a quantum jump in quality and attracted the most attention. This relatively new *appellation* comes under the heading of Coteaux d'Aix-en-Provence, and a majority of its producers are good environmentalists dedicated to growing grapes free from artificial fertilizers, pesticides and herbicides. In Les Baux itself, at the foot of the cliffs, visitors can take a didactic nature walk through the vines of Mas Ste-Berthe (℃ 04 90 54 39 01, ℗ 04 90 54 46 17) and learn all about the grapes.

Before or after lunch, you could go for a wander round the fine houses and shops of **St-Rémy**. Marie has recently opened her culinary boutique, L'Art de la Table, next to the restaurant. Turning left out of the restaurant, you soon come to the diminutive Place Joseph Hilaire, with some tempting-looking food boutiques, the Fromagerie du Mistral selling a beautifully-presented array of Provençal cheeses, the Maison d'Araxie an upmarket grocer's. Down the Rue Carnot you'll find some excellent shops for interior decoration. Wander round the short streets to the north of Rue Carnot to appreciate further tranquil little picturesque squares shaded by *châtaigniers*, chestnut trees.

The Romans had a habit of building monuments and impressive mausolea on the outskirts of their towns, along the main roads. Just a 15-minute walk from the centre of St-Rémy, south on the D5, stand two of the most remarkable Roman relics in France. They were here long before the D5 of course; originally they decorated the end of the Roman road from Arles to Glanum, the ruins of which lie on either side of the modern way. The Triumphal Arch, built probably in the reign of Augustus, was one of the first to be erected in Provence. Its elegant form and marble columns show the Greek sensibility of the artists, far different from the strange Celtic-influenced arches of Orange and Carpentras. In the Middle Ages it inspired the creators of St-Trophime in Arles. Evidently, someone long ago carted off the top for building stone; the slanted tile roof is an 18th-century addition to protect what was left.

Next to it, the so-called Mausoleum was really a memorial to Caesar and Augustus, erected by their descendants in the early 1st century AD. There is nothing else quite like this anywhere, and it is one of the best-preserved of Roman monuments in France. The form is certainly original: a narrow four-faced arch on a solid plinth, surmounted by a cylinder of columns and a pointed roof, 17m above the ground; inside this are statues of Caesar and Augustus. The reliefs on the base are excellent work: mythological scenes including a battle with Amazons,

the Mausoleum
& Municipal Arch

a battle of Greeks and Trojans and a boar hunt. At the top of the arch, you can make out a pair of winged spirits holding a civic crown of laurel—Augustus' symbol for his new political order.

Glanum began as a Celtic settlement—a proper town, really, under a heavy cultural influence from the Greeks at nearby Marseille. The Romans snatched it around 100 BC, under Marius, but not until the great prosperity of the Augustan empire did the city begin to bloom. Almost all of the ruins visible today date from this period. In a prelude to the fall of the Empire, the Franks and Alemanni ranged throughout Gaul in the 250s and 260s. In one of their last hurrahs before the recovering Roman legions drove them out, they sacked Glanum in 270. After that, the townspeople relocated to a healthier and safer site, today's St-Rémy; silt washed down from the Alpilles gradually covered the Roman city, and it passed out of memory until the 19th century, when some accidental finds alerted archaeologists to its presence. Excavations began in 1921, and have since uncovered a fascinating cross-section of Glanum, including its Forum.

The Kingdom of Arles and Daudet-Land

Arles has a majorly serious history for a moderately sized contemporary town. At virtually every stage of the known early story of Provence, up until the medieval period, it figures as an extremely significant settlement. The Celto-Ligurians welcomed the Greeks in the 6th century BC, who made this their major trading post with the locals. Under Provence's Roman hero Marius, a canal was built to connect Arles with the sea. In the civil war between Caesar and Pompey, Marseille foolishly supported the latter. Arles gave Caesar boats to smash its rival and in exchange received the bounty of the lion's share of trade with Rome. Growing in stature through time, in 395 it was declared capital of the 'Three Gauls'—France, Britain and Spain. In the next century, it became the capital of the Visigoths. Christianity then took a firm and splendid grip on the city. From 879 to 1036 it became a capital again, of the territory of Provence-Burgundy, known as the Kingdom of Arles, with lands stretching as far north as Lorraine.

La Cuisine au Planet

Arles boasts several impressive Roman remains: its spectacular amphitheatre, the Roman theatre that still serves, the *cryptoportiques*, vaulted galleries above which the forum was built… Splendid sarcophagi are something of a speciality in Arles, saved in large numbers, not just from the period of the Roman Empire, but also from the Dark Ages. The Alyscamps, one of the most sought-after cemeteries in western Europe in that period, still retains an avenue lined with them.

Van Gogh fell for Arles in a big way, but his failure to persuade his overbearing friend Gauguin to found an artists' colony in the town plunged him into despair and he cut off his ear here. Nobel prize-winning Provençal writer Frédéric Mistral loved Arles and used his prize money to set up the Provençal museum, the Museon Arlaten.

Fontvieille, outside Arles, is where we stop for lunch. It is most famous for the so-called Moulin de Daudet, celebrating the 19th-century writer's short stories, the *Lettres de mon moulin*, a classic of French children's literature, thought to have been partly responsible for bringing Van Gogh to Arles. La Cuisine au Planet, which attracted us, stands in a curious little Fontvieille residential square bordered by houses and, on one side, the Planet, a wall of limestone with caves dug into it. After lunch, we suggest that you go in search of further interesting crumbs of this area's rich cultural legacy, scattered to the east of Arles.

getting there

Fontvieille lies just northeast of Arles up the D17. In the little town, along the main artery, look out for the busy junction with its cafés and a statue of the moustachioed Daudet. Don't take the Avenue des Moulins up to his windmill, but the Route Neuve in the opposite direction. A short distance down this, you come to the Grand Rue. Turn right and you arrive almost immediately on the Place du Planet.

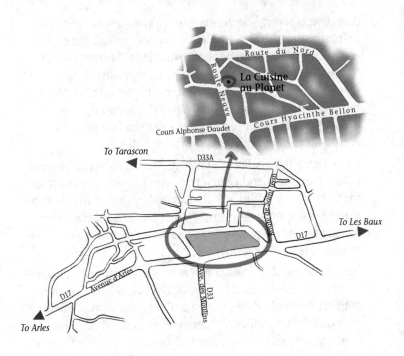

La Cuisine au Planet

La Cuisine au Planet, 144 Grand Rue, 13990 Fontvieille, © 04 90 54 63 97, ☎ 04 90 18 98 09. Closed Mon in winter and Mon lunch and Tues lunch in summer. Closed for holidays a fortnight in Nov and a fortnight in Feb. Menus at 130F and 165F.

The cooking at La Cuisine au Planet is inspired. Philippe Willemet is an interesting culinary mix, Andalucian by birth, Belgian by upbringing, now Provençal by adoption. He trained to become a chef in a leading Belgian *école hôtelière* in Namur. Sent out to cook in the Spanish pavilion at Seville's Expo '92, there he met his Provençal wife, Françoise Fouilly, who looks after you so discreetly during the meal.

The three-course summer menu at 130F was sublime. If you're sensitive about garlic, though, be warned about the little *apéritif* olives

—they're powerful enough to blast further holes in the Planet's limestone rock and could spoil your meal if you don't like them. For starters, our choice was between a *crème froide de courge et poitrine fumée, croûtons au curry* or a *flan de St-Jacques aux coques, sauce au basilic*. The chilled soup looked appealing with its pretty apricot colour and the taste was superlative. The flan was also very subtly flavoured.

There were just a couple of choices for the main course on this cheaper menu. Both were delicious. The duck in the *confit de canard sauce aux griottes* was cooked to perfection, the slightly fatty taste cut by the sharp and sweet cherry sauce. The flick knife provided for the meat seemed unnecessary given its tenderness. The duck was accompanied by a fine *galette* of potatoes in the style of Swiss *rösti* with onions. The grilled salmon showed the first hints of Moorish influences, with its moreish pistachio sauce. An excellent combination, served with a variety of little vegetables.

When it comes to the choice between the cheese platter of goat's and ewe's cheese and the puddings, forget the cheeses here. The puddings are fantastic, the most memorable part of the meal. The *tartelette aux figues* was one of the finest *tartelettes* we have ever tasted in Provence, or anywhere for that matter. Apologies for getting sentimental about a mere tart, but the tempting sound of the pastry and the smell of the warming, honeyed aromas are still vivid to us today. It tasted delicious. All the other puddings were interesting too: a mousse made from almond milk (another touch that could be Moorish); an apple pastry flavoured with aniseed, a *crème brûlée* with cinnamon. Even the sorbet was out of the ordinary, served with a rhubarb *coulis*.

On the more expensive menu, a mere 165F, you get just three courses again, but there is more choice and the food is more luxurious. It is surprising to see *foie gras frais* on such a good-value menu. It is duck *foie gras*, cooked in three vinegars and accompanied by chives. Or, showing an obvious Andalucian touch, there may be red mullet served on a gazpacho. The main courses sounded fairly standard suggestions, but the grilled *loup* (not wolf, but *loup de mer*, sea bass) was cooked in olive oil perfumed with truffles, and the thyme butter melting over the fried *gambas* was given added zest by lemon juice. Garlic, stuffed tomatoes and *ratatouille* accompanied the roast lamb, black olive sauce and potatoes gratinéd with goat's cheese were served with the fillet of beef. All splendidly executed.

In wine terms, you can go for a cheap pitcher of local wine, served by the glass. Among the Coteaux des Baux, we chose the white Terres Blanches, a pleasant wine from the Alpilles, made from grapes that have been biologically produced. Also on offer among the whites is the Château d'Estoublon Mogador. This property's wines have won a couple of medals in the past decade, and the château also produces its own olive oil. You can go and visit it on the D17 road east from Fontvieille heading towards the pretty southern Alpilles village of Maussane.

The food almost made us forget to mention the décor. Out on the tarmac square little trees in pots separate off the restaurant's terrace from the rest of the square. The tables are set with yellow and pink cloths covered with typical Provençal prints. Chic modern lights stand by the tables, and a splendid oleander either side of the entrance. If the weather forces you inside for your meal, the square dining room is appealing, with beams and walls of chunky limestone blocks, poxed by hammer marks.

Tartelette Tiède aux Figues Fraîches Caramélisées

Serve warm with a scoop of vanilla ice cream or custard.

Serves 4

4 circles of puff pastry 4cm/1 ½in in diameter
16 fresh figs
ground cinnamon
granulated sugar

Preheat the oven to 180°C/350°F (gas mark 4). Prick the pastry circles with a fork and place on a lightly greased baking sheet. Bake in the preheated oven for 15 minutes. Remove the pastry cases from the oven and leave to cool, but leave the oven on.

Cut the figs into round slices about 3mm/one-eighth-inch thick and arrange the slices in a circle, overlapping each other, on the pastry circles. Sprinkle with granulated sugar. Bake in the oven for 10 minutes. Remove from the oven and sprinkle each tart with a pinch of cinnamon.

touring around

Like Nîmes, **Arles** has enough intact antiquities to call itself the 'Rome of France'; unlike Nîmes it lingered in the limelight for another 1000 years, producing enough saints for every month on the calendar— Trophimus, Hilarius, Césaire and Genès are some of the more famous. Pilgrims flocked here for a whiff of their odour of sanctity, and asked on their deathbeds to be buried in the holy ground of the Alyscamps. Nowadays Arles holds the distinction of being the largest *commune* in France, ten times larger than Paris, embracing 750 square km of the Camargue and Crau plains; it has given the world the rhythms of the Gypsy Kings, and the pungent joys of *saucisse d'Arles*, France's finest donkey-meat sausage.

Despite the pictures in children's history books, Rome was ruined not so much by tribes of horrid Vandals by the latter-day Romans themselves, who regarded the baths, theatres and temples they inherited as their private stone quarries. The same holds true of Arles's great monuments, except for the amphitheatre or **Arènes** (*open April–Sept 9–7, Oct–Mar 10–4.30*), all of 3m wider than its rival at Nîmes. As enormous as it is, it originally stood another arcade higher, and was clad in marble; as in most public buildings in the Roman empire no expense was spared on its comforts. An enormous awning operated by sailors protected the audience from the sun and rain, and fountains scented with lavender and burning saffron helped cover up the stink of blood spilled by the gladiators and wild animals below. This temple of death survived in good repair because it came in handy. Its walls were tricked out with towers by Saracen occupiers and used as a fortress (like the theatres of Rome), and from the Middle Ages on it sheltered a poor, crime-ridden neighbourhood with two churches and 200 houses, built from stones prised off the amphitheatre's third storey. These were cleared away in 1825, leaving the amphitheatre free for bullfights, and able to pack in 12,000 spectators.

But a different fate was in store for the **Théâtre Antique** (*same hours as Arènes*), just south of the Arènes: in the 5th century, in a fury usually reserved for pagan temples, Christian fanatics pulled it apart stone by stone. A shame, because the fragments of fine sculpture they left in the rubble suggest that the theatre, once also capable of seating 12,000, was much more lavish than the one in Orange. Of the stage, only two tall Corinthian columns survived; they were nicknamed 'the two widows', after being pressed into service as gibbets in the 17th and 18th centuries. The most famous statue of Roman Provence, the Venus of Arles, lay buried at their feet until she was dug up in 1651 and presented to Louis XIV to adorn the gardens of Versailles.

Walk to the Place de la République, an attractive square on the Roman model, with a fountain built around a granite obelisk that once stood in the *spina* (or barrier) of the circus. Overlooking this pagan sun needle is one of the chief glories of Provençal Romanesque style, the **cathedral of St-Trophime**. The original church, built by St Hilaire in the 5th century and dedicated to St Stephen, was rebuilt at the end of the 11th century, and the great portal added in the next. Inspired by the triumphal arches of Glanum and Orange, its reliefs describe the *Last Judgement*, mixing the versions of the *Apocalypse* and *Gospel of Matthew*. As angels blast away on their trumpets, the triumphant Christ sits in majesty in the tympanum, accompanied by the symbols of the four Evangelists, the 12 Apostles, and a gospel choir of 18 pairs of angels. Below, St Michael weighs each soul, separating the good from the evil for their just desserts in the after-life—the fortunate in their long robes are delivered into the bosoms of Abraham, Isaac and Jacob, while the damned, naked and bound like a chain gang, are led off in a conga-line to hell.

After the sumptuous portal, the spartan nudity of the long, narrow nave is as striking as its unusual height (60m). Aubusson tapestries from the 17th century hang across the top, and there are several Palaeochristian sarcophagi along the sides. The best decoration, however, is by a Dutchman named Finsonius, who came down to Arles in

Daudet's mill

1610. Like Van Gogh, he stayed, mesmerized by the light and colour, and met a bad end, drowning in the icy Rhône in 1642. Around the corner in Rue du Cloître is the entrance to St-Trophime's cloister. No other in Provence is as richly and harmoniously sculpted as this, carved in the 12th and 14th centuries by the masters of St-Gilles, a little way west of the Rhône, in the *département* of the Gard.

After lunch at La Cuisine au Planet you could walk to the **Moulin de Daudet**, south on the D33, a rare survivor among the hundreds of windmills that once embellished every hilltop of southern Provence. Alphonse Daudet never really lived here, but his *Lettres de mon moulin*, a collection of sentimental tales of the dying life of rural Provence in the late 1800s, is still popular across France today. The windmill has become a museum of Daudet, with photographs and documents.

Two kilometres south, there are sections of two **Roman aqueducts** that served Arles, along with vestiges of a **Roman mill**, unique in Europe. This huge installation was a serious precursor to the Industrial Revolution, using the flow of the water to power 16 separate mills, along a stretch of canal over a kilometre long; nothing like it has been found anywhere else. It's really something to see; no tourist tic tac, not even a railing. You could simply give Daudet a miss for this.

Just before Arles, the D17 passes one of the most important monasteries of medieval Provence, **Montmajour**. Founded in the 10th century, on what was then almost an island amidst the swamps, this Benedictine abbey was devoted to reclaiming the land, a monumental labour that would take centuries to complete. By the 1300s, the monastery had grown exceedingly wealthy, a real prize for the Avignon popes, who gained control of it and farmed it out, along with its revenues, to friends and relations. Under such absentee abbots, it languished thereafter, and its great church was never completed. Montmajour became a national property not in the Revolution, but five years earlier. The 1786 'Affair of the Diamond Necklace' was a famous swindle that involved both Marie Antoinette and the great charlatan Cagliostro. One of the principal players was Montmajour's abbot, the Cardinal de Rohan; he got caught, and all his property, including the abbey, was confiscated. The abbey did service as a farm-house, and its church as a barn, before restorations began in 1907.

Consequently, there isn't much to see. At the church entrance you'll notice the piers, built into the adjacent wall of the cloister, that would have supported the nave had it been completed. The interior is aus-tere and empty, but gives a good idea of the state of Provençal architecture *c.* 1200, in transition from Romanesque to Gothic. The most interesting part is the lower church, a crypt with an unusual plan, including a long, narrow nave and a circular enclosure under the high altar, with radiating chapels behind it; its purpose has not been explained. The cloister has some fanciful sculptural decoration; see if you can find the camel. Around the back of the church, you'll see a number of tombs cut out of the rock; these are a mystery too, and may predate the abbey. The mighty 26m donjon was built in the 1360s for defence, in that terrible age when the lords of Les Baux and a dozen other hoodlums were tearing up the neighbourhood; next to it, the tiny chapel of St-Pierre (*usually closed*) was the original abbey church, built on the spot where St-Trophime of Arles had his hermitage.

A few hundred yards behind the apse of the church, in the middle of a farm, stands what was the abbey's funeral chapel, Ste-Croix. Don't miss it, even though you'll have to walk through the farmyard muck (it's visible from the road, near a barn). Few buildings show so con-vincingly the architectural sophistication of the Romanesque as this small work of the late 11th century, a central-plan chapel with apses along three sides and an elegant lantern on top.

Eat Mud in the Camargue

For those of you with romantic notions of white horses running freely over the marshlands of the Camargue, black bulls grazing with pure white egrets on their backs and flamingos flying overhead, some words of warning about the Camargue. First, it's heavily touristy. Because of the

church of Notre-Dame at Saintes-Maries-de-la-mer.

large number of *étangs* or lakes, the limited number of roads through the area get clogged up with slow-moving traffic in the holiday season. Second, most of the horses you see look miserable, bored or exhausted, tied in rows to rails by the roadside. Third, along with swarms of tourists, you'll probably find swarms of mosquitoes. These can be a real menace, so take suitable preventive measures.

All in all, if you're not selective, the Camargue can seem rather tatty and disappointing. You should be particularly critical here about what you choose, both in terms of where you eat and the places where you try out Camargue activities like horse-riding or even cattle-ranching. For the unsporty, what makes a visit to the Camargue worthwhile is finding an old-fashioned Spanish-style Camargue *mas*, pastures covered with feisty black bulls, the views from a quiet boat, or seeing a fly-past of flamingos. This is an ornithologists' paradise and if you're interested in birds you should be well satisfied.

The Camargue used to be known to its inhabitants as the *isclo*, the 'island' between the two branches of the Rhône. The Grand Rhône travels from Arles down the eastern side of Camargue. The Petit Rhône meanders its way westwards to the sea, helping to form the western border of Provence. Les Saintes-Maries-de-la-Mer, close to the mouth of the Petit Rhône, is the Camargue's seaside resort and was also once a great place of pilgrimage.

To either side of the Camargue there are contrasting curiosities to visit. To the west, just outside Provence, stand the sturdy fortified walls of Aigues-Mortes, a famous and fabulous French medieval crusaders' port. To the east, still in the Camargue, you can visit the salt dunes outside 19th-century industrial Salin-de-Giraud, one of the most extraordinary culinary landscapes in France.

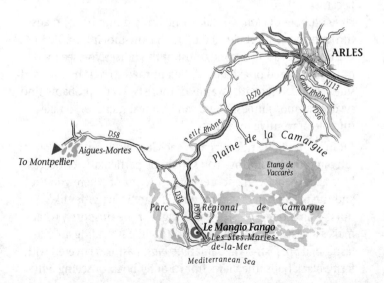

getting there

The Mangio Fango is just 600 metres north of Les Saintes-Maries-de-la-Mer, on the western side of the main D570 to Arles. The house is fairly well hidden but the signs are clear enough.

Le Mangio Fango

Le Mangio Fango, Route d'Arles, 13460 Les Saintes-Maries-de-la-Mer, ✆ 04 90 97 80 56, ✉ 04 90 97 83 60. Closed for holidays 11 Nov–24 Dec and 6 Jan–5 Feb. Menus at 150F, 175F and 195F.

The Mangio Fango is the Provençal nickname for the *mistral*, the eater of mud. The wind can dry the marshland, sucking up its humidity, leaving the crackly earth you may see in summer. The 'i' in the restaurant's title was added by accident, but has stuck idiosyncratically.

Michel Rousselet is the devoted proprietor and chef who has created Le Mangio Fango from scratch. He was actually born in the US, the son of a French diplomat. His cookery training was what he describes as *sur le tas*, that is, on the job. He's been in the Camargue for some 30 years.

Although so close to an uninspiring road, the vegetation at the entrance to Le Mangio Fango immediately distances you from the traffic. You enter what seems like a mini-labyrinth of luxuriant plants, with beyond, a little stretch of green lawn. A horsey smell hangs in the air. You can eat out on the patio, by the outside barbeque giving off more tempting aromas, but the interior is so comfortable and protected that you may prefer to stay inside. To deal with the unwelcome guests on Camargue evenings, mosquitoes, the patio has been treated.

The house, typically whitewashed Camargue, has a Spanish or Mexican feel. You can eat either downstairs or on the gallery above. The décor is definitely soigné, clean and chic. You could take an *apéritif* on the huge rounded-edged wicker chairs by the fireplace, with a chessboard in the chimney and its two cross-beams holding pots and Camargue *gardians'* spurs and branding irons. Various decoy ducks are perched around the place. Other curious and interesting objects around the room attract the attention, such as elongated lampshades or the boat and heads in pottery on the bull-black surface of the piano.

Not surprisingly, guitar music was playing—the Camargue is the territory of the Gypsy Kings.

The cuisine concentrates on the *saveurs de la mer*, the flavours of the sea. An appropriate start to the meal would be the *tellines du Golfe de Beauduc*, shells scarcely bigger than finger nails. They are served in such a delicious *aïoli* sauce that you'll want to lick every single one, and it took quite some time to get through the whole platter. This very fine-tasting shell is practically an exclusivity of Provence, normally just served with a *persillade*. On the 175F three-course menu you could start with the fisherman's soup or, real ducks featuring several times on the menu, the *terrine de colvert*, served with a *compote* of onions.

The *plat de combat* of the Camargue is Camargue bull stew. To be found on virtually every menu in the area, it can be very disappointing, tough and mouth-drying. M. Rousselet prepares it tenderly as *daube de taureaux des gardians*, in Lirac wine, the latter from nearby on the west bank of the Rhône. We actually chose a rosé for the meal, a Mas de Rey Cuvée Prestige Van Gogh, a vin de pays des Bouches du Rhône, which comes with a Van Gogh self-portrait on the label and a warm invitation to visit the property.

For 195F you get a four-course menu, which includes the cheese course. Among the hors d'oeuvre, you might have been tempted by mussels with a Provençal sauce or the famous Provençal dish, *bouill-abaisse*, here served in jelly. Go for one of the fish dishes as a main course, either monkfish medallions or Mediterranean sea bass in a *beurre blanc* with a flash of lemon. If the *bourride* fish soup is available, try that. However, the duck *magret* is, like much of the fish, grilled on the wood fire and may be served with a green pepper sauce and delicious morel mushrooms.

Chocolate features prominently on the dessert list to the joy of chocoholics. The choice of tarts is wide too. The *tarte amandine au citron* is a delicious almond and lemon tart. Or you might be tempted by a soufflée tart with peaches. For hotter days, try the *vacherin aux marrons*, an ice-cream pudding with chestnuts.

Le Grand Aïoli

Serve this aïoli with warm vegetables—carrots, turnips, potatoes and cauliflower—, cooked until just done, hard-boiled eggs, salt cod and escargots de mer, if you like them, for a typically Provençal meal that is easy to make. Note that if you add a little saffron, this aïoli goes well with fish soup or bouillabaisse.

Serves 6

12 garlic cloves
500ml/17fl oz of oil (olive oil or groundnut oil, or a
*   combination of the two according to taste)*
3 egg yolks, no trace of white
pinch of fine salt
pinch of finely ground pepper

Peel the garlic cloves and blend them in a food processor with 200ml/7fl oz of the oil. Put the 3 raw egg yolks in a bowl with the salt and pepper. Incorporate the garlic and oil mixture, bit by bit, into the egg yolks by beating, as you would for a mayonnaise. Add the rest of the oil in the same way. Your mixture should now have the same consistency as mayonnaise.

---

touring around

Start the day with a visit to splendidly defended **Aigues-Mortes** above the lakes of the Petite Camargue. Every French history or geography schoolbook has a photo of Aigues-Mortes in it, and every Frenchman, most likely, carries in his mind the haunting picture—the great walls of the port where Louis IX, alias St Louis, sailed off to the Crusades in the mid-13th century. The town is now marooned in the muck of the advancing Rhône delta. It is as compelling a symbol of time and fate as any Roman ruin, and as magically evocative of medieval France as any Gothic cathedral.

Forgotten and nearly empty a century ago, Aigues now makes its living from tourists, and from salt; a large percentage of France's supply is collected here, at the enormous Salins-du-Midi pans south of town. Aigues-Mortes's walls are over a mile in length, streamlined and almost perfectly rectangular. The impressive Tour de Constance is a huge cylindrical defence tower that guarded the northeastern land approach to the town (*entry inside the walls on Rue Zola; open daily 9.30–12 and 2–4.30 in winter, 9–7 in summer; adm*).

Aigues-Mortes isn't very large, so you may well find you have time to go and look at **Les Saintes-Maries-de-la-Mer** before lunch. Set among low sand-dunes, this jovial and lively town has an open-armed approach to visitors that long predates any interest in the Camargue and its ecological balance. For this is one of Provence's holy of holies, and if you come out of season you become aware of the dream-like, insular remoteness that made it the stuff of legend.

The pious story behind it all was promoted to the hilt by the medieval Church: after Christ was crucified, his Jewish detractors took a boat without sails or oars and loaded it with three Marys—Mary Salome (mother of the apostles James and John), Mary Jacobe, the Virgin's sister, and Mary Magdalene, along with the Magdalene's sister Martha and their resurrected brother Lazarus, and St Maximin and St Sidonius. As this so-called Boat of Bethany drifted off shore, Sarah, the black Egyptian servant of Mary Salome and Mary Jacobe, wept so grievously at being left behind that Mary Salome tossed her cloak on the water, so that Sarah was able to walk across on it and join the saints. The boat took them to the Camargue, to this spot where the elderly Mary Salome, Mary Jacobe and Sarah built an oratory, while their younger companions went to spread the Gospel, live in caves, and tame Tarasques, Rhône river monsters. In 1448, during the reign of Good King René (who was always pinched for money) the supposed relics of the two Marys were discovered, greatly boosting the local pilgrim trade. Les Saintes-Maries became, as Mistral called it, the 'Mecca of Provence'. Most famously, gypsies, who claim Sarah to be one of their own, made it one of their great places of pilgrimage, which it has remained. They flock here at the end of May.

The 12th-century church of Les Saintes-Maries is, along with St-Victor in Marseille, the most impressive fortified church in Provence: a crenellated ship with loopholes for windows, long at anchor in a small pond of white villas with orange roofs. Inside, along the gloomy nave, are wells that supplied the church-fortress in times of siege;

pilgrims still bottle the water to ensure their protection by St Sarah. In the second chapel on the left, near the model of the Boat of Bethany that is carried in the pilgrimage procession to the sea, is the polished rock 'pillow' of the saints, discovered with their bones in 1448. The capitals supporting the blind arches of the raised choir are finely sculpted in the style of St-Trophime in Arles. Under the choir is the crypt, where the relics and statue of St Sarah in her seven robes are kept; the statue has been kissed so often that the black paint has come off in patches. Here, too, is a *taurobolium*, or relief of a bull-slaying from an ancient *mithraeum*, the bits scratched away long ago by women who used the dust to concoct fertility potions, along with photos and ex votos left by the gypsies. From April to mid-November, you can climb to below the bell tower to appreciate the views stretching across the Camargue (*open 10–12.30 and 2.30–7*).

The Mangio Fango can give you information on how to become a Camargue cowboy or cowgirl for the day, as well as on all sorts of other activities. You could try one of these after lunch. Horse-riding is extremely popular. M. Rousselet recommends the Promenade Lou Sagnas, 200m from the hotel, through which you can book. The rides last two hours or more, and you can discover the marshlands and lakes nearby. Beginners are welcome. You might feel more comfortable on a bike. You can rent one from the Mangio Fango if you're staying there, or go to the Vélo Saintois in Les Saintes-Marie (*© 04 90 97 74 56 or 04 90 97 81 45; half-day minimum*).

You may be tempted to go on a four-wheel drive tour of a Camargue estate accompanied by one of the rare remaining professional *manadiers* or *gardians*, the Camargue's real 'cowboys'. You need to organize such an outing well in advance. M. Rousselet recommends M. Arnaud of the Manade Gilbert Arnaud (14 rue des Launes, Les Saintes-Maries-de-la-Mer, *© 04 90 97 99 20, @ 04 90 97 78 06*—or go via the Mangio Fango). M. Rousselet describes M. Arnaud as a serious guide, who will teach you about the life of the *gardians*, about their activities looking after the herds, and about the fragile ecosystem of the area.

Another option that allows you to experience the Camargue in depth would be to take a boat trip with Les Barques de Camargue (*© 06 09*

95 53 83). You go in exclusive groups of six or eight people on a motorized boat with a guide. Much more touristy, there's a choice of boats which will take you up the Petit Rhône close to the restaurant, such as the *Tiki*, the *Quatre Maries*, the *Camargue* or the *Soleil*. The captains comment along the way. These boats tend to go as far as the bac du Sauvage, where a mini ferry takes cars across the Petit Rhône during the day. This might amuse the children, but be warned that the ferry stops operating during lunch hours and queues quickly build up for the last crossing before mealtime. Most of the cars have to turn back. So don't use this ferry crossing coming from Aigues-Mortes if you're late for lunch at the Mangio Fango.

You may want to concentrate more on the **natural world** and history of the Camargue. Several sites circling the Etang de Vaccarès focus on these aspects. In terms of birds and plants, first and most spectacularly, there are the flamingos (*flamants roses*); several thousand of them nest around the southern lagoons. Probably no place in the Mediterranean has a wider variety of aquatic birds: lots of ducks, grebes, cormorants, curlews and ibis. The little egret is a common sight, though it spends the winter in Africa, as does the avocet, which looks like an aquatic magpie. There are also many purple herons, conspicuously striped on the head and breast. Not all the birds are aquatic; you may see an eagle or a majestic red kite (*milan royal*).

Nearest to the Mangio Fango, at Pont de Gau on the road to Arles, you'll find a **Parc ornithologique** (*open 9–sunset, Feb–Nov 9.30–sunset*), with aviaries for wounded birds and walking paths, followed by a Centre d'Information du Parc de la Camargue (*open summer 9–6, winter 9.30–5; closed Fri, Oct–Mar*) with small exhibitions and viewing telescopes.

Continuing towards Arles, four km beyond Albaron along the D570, the Mas du Pont de Rousty has been transformed into the **Musée de la Camargue** (*open daily exc Tues, 10–4.15; April–Sept daily 9.15–6.45*). It was an inspiration on the part of the Regional Park management to create this museum in what was not long ago a working Camargue cattle and sheep ranch. There are special exhibits on the *gardians*, on the fickle Rhône (you'll learn that 400,000 years ago it flowed past Nîmes), on Mistral's love-maddened *Miréio*, and other subjects.

Outside, marked nature trails lead deep into the surrounding swampy plain, the Marais de la Grande Mar.

Go back down past Albaron and take the D37 to circle the Etang de Vaccarès. Switch onto the D36B down the eastern edge. The **Centre d'Information La Capelière** (*open daily 9–12 and 2–7*), with exhibits on flora and fauna, also proposes fascinating guided nature walks around the lagoon.

Industrial **Salin-de-Giraud** by the Grand Rhône comes as a bit of a surprise, with its industrial workers' blocks of flats from the 19th century, built for salt and soap workers. Not far to the east of course lies the massive 20th-century industrial landscape of the Port de Fos. Take the D36D out of Salin to go and see the dunes of salt produced here, an amazing sight even for children with no interest in the culinary. You can drive your car or cycle to the top of a mound which allows you better views over the billions of grains of salt and the network of salt pans beyond. This is apparently the largest saltworks in Europe and it is staggering. It covers some 110 square kilometres, producing around 800,000 tonnes of salt a year. The seawater is simply left to evaporate, leaving salt which is collected into pyramids called *camelles*.

Find the track for **Beauduc**, a reasonable distance winding directly west of Salin (follow signs for the Plage de Beauduc or the restaurants named below). You could stop by the Etang du Fangassier, where the *gardes flamants* have a lookout post to survey from April to mid-July the 10,000 couples of flamingos sojourning in the Camargue. Continue to Beauduc, a run-down village of shacks, said by locals to lie at the end of the earth—electricity lines haven't even managed to reach this far. In the evening you could happily eat grilled fish at Chez Juju or at Marc et Mireille and enjoy the views of the pretty bay with the odd fishing boat bobbing about. This is what a visit to the Camargue is all about.

Nostradamus Predicts an Excessively Good Restaurant for You in Salon-de-Provence

Nostradamus wrote the bulk of his star-gazing predictions, the enormously enigmatic *Centuries*, in Salon-de-Provence. Ever since then pundits of all kinds have tried to foresee the future of our world through them. Their deluded attempts are bound to fail because Nostradamus's quatrains may be astrological in part, but in others they're extremely poetic and often gobbledegook. But Nostradamus is a learned 16th-century character worthy of serious consideration.

It's not just because of the lunatic interpretations of its most famous inhabitant's writings that Salon has something of a poisoned reputation. Its prized olive oil was much later exploited by the land-owners around here to make fine soap and fortunes off the backs of the cowed labour force. And today Salon's air force base and its screeching planes hardly draw a positive reaction from outsiders. Many guidebooks turn their backs on Salon, dismissing it as ugly, dull and

La Salle à manger

unattractively modernized. Come in from the outskirts and you may be pleasantly surprised, even enchanted.

Salon's dark-shaded main string of boulevards slithers along under heavy plane tree foliage and past mossy fountains, a deeply attractive snake of streets. Our restaurant lies just to the side of it.

One of the main complaints levelled at Salon is the ruthless postwar replacement of this heart. True, the surgery does look botched in parts. And one problem with the new modern Place des Centuries is that the replacement hasn't managed to pump the expected life back into Salon.

If you're still dissatisfied by a morning in Salon, for the afternoon we propose the simpler Provençal pleasures of the village of Eyguières to the northwest, the touristic château and zoo of La Barben just to the east, or, most reluctantly, as this is one of our favourite spots in Provence and surprisingly little known, the village of Vernègues. Its high, ruined castle plateau commands breathtaking views in all directions over the Bouches-du-Rhône and up to the Montagne de Lubéron.

getting there

Midway between Avignon and Marseille, Salon-de-Provence lies close to the A7 motorway. The splendid set of plane-shaded *cours* already mentioned serpenting through the centre of town is one-way. You'll come up the Cours Victor Hugo, with its great mossy fountain at the bottom. Soon you turn left off the *cours* and the restaurant is at the start of the Rue Maréchal Joffre.

La Salle à Manger

La Salle à Manger, 6 Rue du Maréchal Joffre, 13300 Salon-de-Provence,
℗ 04 90 56 28 01. Closed Sun pm and Mon, and for holidays 5–25 Aug
and 23 Dec–5 Jan. Menus at 89F and 125F. Add about 35F for pudding.

You may have been attracted by the type of prosperous 19th-century residential façade that typifies the houses in the streets immediately

To Avignon

N538

Bd Ledru-Rollin

Boulevard Coren

Boulevard Nostradamus

Place du
Général de Gaulle

Bd J F Kennedy

Rue Joliot

Boulevard David

Boulevard Lamartine

La Salle à Manger

Cours Victor Hugo

To Arles

Boulevard de la République

Cours Carnot

Rue de l'Horloge

Place de
L'Hotel
de Ville

To Vernègues

Château
de l'Empéri

Place des
Centuries

Boulevard des Copachu

Boulevard Maréchal Foch

Cours Gimon

Rue Lafayette

Boulevard J Jaures

Rue du Tech

Boulevard Victor Hugo

Place Morgan

Boulevard du Roi René

Allée de Craponne

N538

To Arles &
Marseille

beyond Salon's historic kernel. Now you can get the chance to see inside one. Step through the front door of La Salle à Manger and you enter an undeniably charming Salon scene. Rather than just a dining room, as you might imagine to go by the restaurant's name, this is in fact a whole, typical Belle Epoque house. It has all the gaiety associated with the successful bourgeoisie of that period. M. Miège describes it as a *maison de maître*, a family mansion, dating from the end of the 19th century. The entrance wall painting gives some indication of the excesses to come.

You could eat in the enclosed, bright courtyard outside, overlooked by a chestnut tree, but its decoration is rather basic by contrast with the wild décor within. The restored wall paintings of the *salle à manger* itself make such an impression that you may well prefer to plump for it even on a fine summer day. Great bouquets of painted flowers splash colours over several panels, musical instruments sometimes thrown into their midst.

Angels float about above, while the elaborate ceiling mouldings are picked out in mushroom and gilt colours. Palms add to the exotic feel. Flower patterns are repeated on the tiles. Of course such decoration is bound to become ridiculous to some extent and there are some added lapses of taste, for example the hideous Polynesian statue. But the dining room is still captivating. The waiter and waitress, the bubbly children of the owners Elyane and Francis Miège, who have emigrated south from Normandy, matched the interiors with their floral dress and waistcoat.

The *salle à manger*'s extravagance cries out to you to drink a cocktail. We tried the restaurant's special Lou Parpaillon, a drink in honour of le bon roi René, almond liquor mixed with a lightly sparkling Muscat Beaumes-de-Venise. Probably only for the sweet-toothed, but delicious and aromatic. On closer inspection, our glasses were engraved with more flowers and with birds.

The menus are somewhat excessive, to say the least. Even their presentation is in keeping. One year they were covered with fairy-tale scenes. Another year, with sugary-sweet old advertising calendar pages, one hilariously inappropriately promoting corned beef above a pink-cheeked and pink-dressed *bergère* or shepherdess. (Incidentally, Salon boasts the Ecole de Bergers, France's national school for shepherds!)

On to the serious contents of the menus. Given the elaborate surroundings, you won't be surprised to hear that virtually nothing on the menu is simple. Each dish is devoted a couple of lines of description. The choices of starters and main courses (125F for the two) is enormous. Were you an air force pilot in a rush you might think of bolting down the weekday lunchtime menu express at 89F, where the choice of starter and main course is made for you.

On the expensive menu there are ten starters to choose from. Some may be alarmingly unfamiliar, such as *la fleur de piquillos à la brandade de Nîmes, sauce aïoli glacée* (*piquillos* are little peppers, not too hot). You will need to concentrate on studying the menu, and would in fact do best to come armed with a multi-volume French dictionary to assist you as several of the words are extremely obscure. At times the dishes sound like recipes concocted by a French answer to Edward Lear (try working out, for instance, *le gaspacho à la rémoulade de supions, coriandre fraîche et poudre d'Espelette* or *la bisquebouille de petits coquillages en fines ravioles, bouillon d'écrevisses, pulpe de melon et curcuma*).

The *paupiette d'aubergine au confit de lapereau sur une fondue de tomates au pistou* consisted of the tenderest of aubergines with the tenderest little pieces of rabbit served with a tomato sauce—delicious if you can put Beatrix Potter out of your mind. We appreciated the *tartine de rougets en escabèche* so much that we requested it without hesitation as the recipe to be included in this book. There may even be the possibility of carpaccio of bison or of ostrich, and you should be able to order a *vol au vent aux grenouilles!*

With the main courses, again there is a choice of ten. *Béquet*, by the way, is the bit above the *gigot* or lamb's leg, here rubbed with garlic, peppered with pieces of rosemary and served with a moussaka *à la provençale*. For another typical strong Provençal taste, you might have gone boldly for the *magret de canard empégué de pastis aux herbes—empégué* is a Provençal word for drunken. The Normandy Miège family has clearly adapted happily to Mediterranean ways. The fresh cod came covered in chorizo sausage scales, served with Camargue rice. Among other elaborate fish dishes on the menu were monkfish poached in smoked milk and sea bream baked with citrus zest and served in a ginger butter. Everything we tried was extremely tasty, but some of the dishes are not for the faint-hearted, so choose according to your known preferences, or be prepared to jump into unknown realms of the palate.

The excess of La Salle à Manger, fit for a Marie Antoinette in the making, is perhaps at its most obvious in the absurdly large choice of puddings, 40 listed in all on the separate menu of '40 desserts Grand-Mère'! Numerous traditional chocolate puddings and *charlottes* feature here. Or you could opt for a chilled tart or for one that's flamboyantly flambéd. Then again there are different kinds of ice creams. You come to realize that the restaurateur is enjoying a bit of a joke with the pudding menu. It's more a good choice of fillings that is being offered for a much smaller number of classic French puddings than 40 distinct desserts. But it typifies this jolly, delightful, enjoyably excessive restaurant.

La Tartine de Rougets en Escabèche

Serve on slices of toasted pain de campagne with salad—rocket is especially good.

Serves 4

10 coriander seeds
5 or 6 sprigs fresh coriander
12 garlic cloves
1 onion
2 carrots
800g/1lb 10oz red mullet fillets
400ml/14fl oz olive oil
400ml/14fl oz cider vinegar
bouquet garni
150ml/¼ pint water
25 saffron pistils
pinch of cayenne pepper
salt and pepper

Crush the coriander seeds and chop the fresh coriander. Peel and slice the garlic, onion and carrots finely.

Wash the mullet fillets. Warm 4 tablespoons of the olive oil in a pan, fry the mullet fillets over a high heat, then drain on some absorbent paper. Place them side by side in a terrine.

Pour 5 tablespoons of the olive oil into a pan and cook the carrots, onion and garlic in it. Add the vinegar and bouquet garni and simmer until reduced by a half.

Add the water, the rest of the oil, the coriander seeds, fresh coriander, saffron pistils, cayenne pepper and salt and pepper to taste and mix. Bring to the boil, then leave to cook for 3 minutes.

Pour the mixture into the terrine over the mullet fillets and leave to marinate for 2 or 3 days in the fridge.

---

touring around

The best way to enter the old heart of **Salon** is by the great 18th-century Porte de l'Horloge, crowned by a typical Provençal iron-work clock tower. It's not possible to have missed this gateway coming into town, as the one-way system forces you to come past it. Nor can you help noticing the vast mural of a sage, bearded, French Renaissance male face. Yes, you've guessed, it portrays Nostradamus of course. Walking down the Rue de l'Horloge, you'll come to the Rue Nostradamus on the left. On this you'll find the **Maison Nostradamus** (*open 2–6, exc Tues*), which consists of a series of little rooms following Nostradamus's intellectual development through static waxworks scenes and slightly complex recorded French commentaries.

Salon's most famous citizen was born in St-Rémy in 1503, to a family of converted Jews. Trained as a doctor in Montpellier, young Michel de Nostredame made a name for himself by successfully treating plague victims in Lyon and Aix. In 1547, he married a girl from Salon and settled down here, practising medicine and pursuing a score of other interests besides—studying astrology, publishing almanacs and inventing new recipes for cosmetics, hair dyes and curative *confitures* or jams. The first of his *Centuries*, ambiguous quatrains written in the future tense, were published in 1555, achieving celebrity for their author almost immediately.

Nostradamus himself said that his works came from 'natural instinct and poetic passion'; in form they are similar to some other poetry of the day, such as the *Visions* of du Bellay. It may be that he had never really intended to become an occult superstar—but when the peasants start bringing you two-headed sheep, asking for an explanation, and when the Queen Regent of France sends an invitation to court, what's a man to do? Nostradamus went to Paris, and later Charles IX and Catherine de' Medici came to visit him in Salon. The Salonnais didn't appreciate such notoriety; if it hadn't been for Nostradamus's royal favour, they might well have put him to the torch. In the bookshop-cum-entrance hall to the Maison Nostradamus you can find sensible books on Nostradamus and by Nostradamus, including not just his *Centuries*, but also his healing jam recipes.

Next we stepped inside the Carpe Diem **librairie ésotérique** (esoteric bookshop) near the Maison Nostradamus. The slickly charming Belgian who runs it says he was called here by supernatural forces. There was much talk of turning the *pierre brute* into the *pierre philosophale*, not transgressing the *ordre cosmique*, looking at the *ultime numéro* 12, various *degrés solaires de naissance* (birth), and ways of decoding of the contents of our *atomes-germes* by tarot cards. Sceptical? Still, several anxious-to-desperate looking individuals walked in while we were there, clearly seeking some solace in this place. And the Belgian explained modestly that he had predicted the results of the 1995 French elections very accurately.

Go past the Eglise St-Michel nearby, built of beautiful fudge-coloured blocks and decorated with some worn but characterful stone carvings, into the **Place des Centuries**, the square that has attracted so much wrath. But is it really that bad? Many have an aesthetic problem with concrete, which does dominate, but there is imagination evident in some of the modern buildings, with battlement-like sloping walls at their bases and sharply angled windows. The square's main problem is that it lacks cafés and bustle. However, we can recommend the little restaurant Le Regain on the square. It may not have the immediate charm of La Salle à Manger, but it's a pleasant little place. While the décor is slightly sterile, the dishes burst with the flavours of Provence and are extremely good value.

Above the square stands the impressively solid **Château de l'Empéri**. Long a possession of the archbishops of Arles, parts of it go back to the 10th century. The **Musée de l'Empéri** (*open daily exc Tues, 10–12 and 2.30–6.30*) set around courtyards with cannons, contains a substantial hoard of weapons, military bric-a-brac and epauletted mannequins on horseback, covering the evolution of France's army and French warfare from Louis XIV to 1918. The star of the show here is mesmerizingly nasty Napoleon.

In the afternoon we escape from Salon. **Eyguières**, north of the town along the D17, has many of the attractions you expect from a Provençal village, Celtic-Greek tombs above the ruins of a medieval castle, fountains bringing life to the streets. The **Château de la Barben**, east of Salon along the D572, is more touristy, the grounds of the château (a fort turned elegant stately home, once owned by Napoleon's sister Pauline Borghese) containing a zoo.

Vernègues, by contrast, is largely ignored. Take the little D16 northeast up into the hills above Salon. Abandoned terraced fields reveal from afar that it has known more prosperous times. In the lower village you could go and see the handful of craftspeople at work. You need to leave your car half way up the hillside to reach the ruins of the château. You can take little rocky tracks up; watch your step and try not to damage the hillside flora too much. At the top, behind the few broken walls of the castle that still stand, the great plateau is often viciously whipped by the wind. The scarce trees here seem to have died in twisted torment. Walk across the plateau and you can climb the rickety, rusty steps up to a tower with a *table d'orientation*. This signals the spectacular mountains you can see in so many directions: the Lubéron to the north, the Alpilles to the west, on a good day, the Montagne Ste-Victoire to the east, and to the south, the massive cliffs that fall into the sea by Marseille.

A Haven in the Port of Marseille

Marseille, France's second largest city, is one hell of a big mess of a metropolis. In the media it has a dirty reputation. The French mafia or *milieu*'s activities, rampant racism, murder, foul play in the venerated and absurdly expensive football team, l'Olympique de Marseille (l'OM for short), frequently make the national headlines, all giving the city a bad boy reputation. But despite this catalogue of problems, central Marseille is brilliantly vibrant and stunningly beautiful in parts.

Marseille's bay seduced the Greeks into setting up their first French trading post here. Today, monster ships dock at the port on the western side, the industrial plants shimmering in silvery sunshine. Hulking ferry boats sail off south into the Mediterranean, towards Corsica or North Africa. The breathtaking bay opens out to the east. In between, the Vieux Port in the urban centre is crammed with the thickest forest of masts imaginable, boats weaving their way in and out.

There are museums and sites galore to engross you in Marseille, but if the urban pace overwhelms you, you could try heading east for the massive cliffs and the *calanques*, the narrow coastal creeks that have cut into the towering rockface.

the Vieux Port, Marseilles

getting there

The Vieux Port is one of the easiest spots to find in Marseille. In fact, it's the centre of town. Chez Brun lies almost exactly opposite the town hall, on the other, southern side of the yacht harbour. Keep an eye out for the entrance, though, which isn't obvious. The restaurant shuns publicity, perched up a sloping, slightly treacherous stairway. Only a discreet plaque down in the street indicates its entrance.

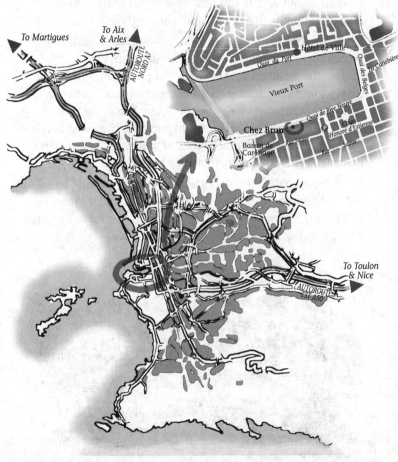

A Haven in the Port of Marseille

Chez Brun

Chez Brun, 2ème Etage, 18 Quai Rive Neuve, 13007 Marseille, ☎ 04 91 33 35 38, 📠 04 91 33 05 69. Closed Sun and Mon lunch and a fortnight in mid-Aug. Lunchtime meal, including wine, at 220F; evening meal at 280F without wine.

The big window at one end of Chez Brun looks out from its second-storey height over the Vieux Port and across to the diminutive old town hall, almost obscured by the mass of masts in the way. Some six church spires were visible from our window-side spot. But even if you don't get one of the few window seats the décor will provide you with plenty to absorb your attention. And anyway you might not particularly like to look out onto some of what we saw. Apart from the *mairie* and the churches, the war-bombed buildings of the Vieux Port were replaced by simple horizontal-sliced modern blocks after the Second World War. And during our lunch we watched in amazement as a desperate prostitute outrageously obviously tried to pick up trade at the bar down below on the pavement, her little girl in tow. On the other side of the road some absurdly expensive yachts bobbed in the water by Marseille's exclusive yacht club, the Société Nautique. It was hard not to think of the endless connections made between extravagance and exploitation in those urban crime thrillers that are such an obsession of Western cinema and television. In our pathetic scene the cliché of the screen seemed appallingly brought to life.

Chez Brun is a haven in a rough city. It's perched calmly above the crowds: no brash street façade or self-advertisement, no billboard crying out for attention. In fact, there is seemingly no sign at all to indicate the restaurant, except that plaque to indicate a professional's offices, but in this case not a lawyer's or a doctor's, but a chef's. Read the plaque and it refers elegantly to *mets provençaux*, Provençal dishes. Take the steep sloping steps up to the little carving at the top, which has something of the appearance of a shrine. Ring on the bell to the right and enter.

At Chez Brun you do feel that cuisine is being treated as a noble profession. The Solamitos, who run the restaurant, are gentle and kind. Raoul Solamito wanders round in a white chef's coat, but in fact the chief cook is a young and talented Spaniard, Marcelo Onzalez, who trained under M. Maximin, one of the great French chefs, of the Negresco in Nice. Mme. Solamito may well be standing at the delightful counter, with its hundreds of compartments, when you arrive. A wonderful spiral staircase leads up to the left to a raised gallery of a dining room suffused with apricot light thanks to the colour of the draperies hung overhead. The restaurant has an excellent atmosphere, southern and spacious.

In some Provençal restaurants you're not given a choice of starters; a whole selection of them is forced upon you. This is the case at Chez Brun with its lunchtime menu. It costs 220F for the four courses. This is expensive, but the price includes a *pichet* or jug of red or rosé Coteaux d'Aix wine. The little hors d'oeuvre dishes are utterly wonderful. They include *pissaladière* (the Provençal version of pizza), *foie de volaille*, two types of *tapenade*, *saucisson d'Arles*, *tomates farcies*, *pan bagna*, *échalotes confites*, *beurre aux poivrons*, *croûtons*...even the home-made chips to accompany all this were delicious. Although there is a predominance of garlic, onions and shallots, there is something to please everyone.

The wall decorations rather resemble the starters in being a great mix of disparate elements. Paintings of Provençal scenes and Provençal personalities include one of the man after whom the restaurant is named, the late M. Brun, identifiable in glasses. M. and Mme. Solamito moved in two years ago, from just next door. Their portraits do not feature on the wall, but Mistral and Nostradamus are there.

For the main course we could choose between tuna on potato slices and a *cassoulet* of seashells. The tuna steaklets showed what a fine fish this can be, especially served in thin slices, rather than as a thick steak. The change in texture to the potato base made an excellent contrast. The *cassoulet de coquillages* had plenty of meaty shell food and masses of delicious sauce to be lapped up. The cooking is truly excellent.

The cheese is a fixed course like the hors d'oeuvre, a tangy goat's cheese on a bed of salad with plenty of chives. Pudding wasn't the traditional gazpacho, but a gazpacho of melon with fresh figs. A brilliant combination and surely a dessert you could whisk up quite easily at home. It was accompanied by melon sorbet and tasted meltingly enjoyable. We took our time over coffee, enjoying Chez Brun's elevated atmosphere before heading back out into the urban jungle.

Escalopes de Thon avec Pommes de Terre Fondantes et Salicornes, Crème de Poireaux

Serves 4

4 new potatoes, thickly sliced
7 ½ tablespoons olive oil
750ml/1 ¼ pints fish or vegetable stock
3 leeks, finely sliced
2 garlic cloves, crushed
sprig thyme
salt and pepper
12 slices fresh tuna, each about 50g/2oz
1 handful fresh samphire or spinach leaves

Preheat the oven to 220°C/425°F (gas mark 7). Fry the potato slices gently on each side in 1 tablespoon of the oil in a casserole dish until they become golden brown. Cover with 200ml/7fl oz of the stock and sprinkle ½ tablespoon of the olive oil over. Bake in the preheated oven until the liquid has evaporated. Transfer to plates and set aside, keeping them warm.

In a frying pan, brown the leeks with the garlic cloves and sprig of thyme in 1 tablespoon of the oil. Moisten with the rest of the stock and leave to cook very gently, covered, for 25 minutes. Mix, pass through a fine sieve and season to taste with salt and pepper. Remove the sauce from the heat and keep warm.

Just before serving, heat 2 tablespoons of the olive oil and fry each slice of tuna, being careful not to overcook them. On each plate place the slices of tuna on the potatoes.

Lightly fry the samphire in 1 tablespoon of the oil and sprinkle over the tuna. Place 2 tablespoons of the sauce around the sides of the tuna and potatoes on each plate, and sprinkle a little of the remaining oil over each portion. Serve immediately.

touring around

Marseille the urban mangrove entwines its aquatic roots around the neat, rectangular **Vieux Port**, where people have lived continuously for the past 2600 years. A little foot-passenger ferry links the two sides of the Vieux Port, going from almost in front of Chez Brun to the town hall. Now a pleasure port, the Vieux Port's cafés have fine views of the sunset, though in the morning the action and smells centre around the Quai des Belges and its boat-side fish market, where the key ingredients of *bouillabaisse*, Marseille's great fish dish, are touted in a racy *patois* as thick as the soup itself. From the Quai des Belges *vedettes* sail to the Château d'If and Frioul islands, past the two bristling fortresses that still defend the harbour. A bronze marker in the Quai des Belges pinpoints the spot where the Greeks first set foot in Gaul.

North of the Vieux Port lies the **Panier** ('the Basket', named after a 17th-century cabaret), Marseille's oldest quarter, an irregular weave of winding narrow streets and stairs, many in the perpetual shadow of steep houses and flapping laundry. When the well-to-do moved out in the 18th century, the Panier was given over to fishermen and a romanticized underworld. Before the war it was a lively Corsican and Italian neighbourhood, and later its warren of secret ways absorbed hundreds of Jews and other refugees from the Nazis, hoping to escape to America. In January 1943, Hitler cottoned on and, in collusion with local property speculators, ordered the dynamiting of everything between the Vieux Port and halfway up the hill, to the Grand'Rue/Rue Caisserie. Given one day to evacuate, the 20,000 departing residents were screened by French and German police, who selected 3500 for the concentration camps. A monument in the quarter commemorates the destruction and deportees who never returned.

Only a handful of buildings were protected from the dynamite, including the 17th-century Hôtel de Ville on the quay, and behind it, in Rue de la Prison, the Maison Diamantée, Marseille's 16th-century Mannerist masterpiece, named after the pyramidical points of its façade. It holds the **Musée du Vieux Marseille** (*open daily 10–5 winter, 11–6 summer*), a delightful attic where the city stashes its odds and ends—Provençal furniture; an extraordinary relief diorama made in

1850 by an iron merchant, depicting the uprising of 1848; 18th-century Neapolitan Christmas crib figures and *santons* made in Marseille; playing and tarot cards, long an important local industry; and poignant photos of the Panier before it was blown to smithereens.

Once you walk north of Rue Caisserie, the Panier retains some of its old character in the web of lanes atop the steps of Montée des Accoules, and around Place de Lenche, the former *agora* of the Greeks. Just to the north, looming over the tankers and cargo ships drowsing in Marseille's outer harbour basin, are the two 'majors'. The striped neo-Byzantine **Cathédrale de la Major** (*closed Mon and 12–2*) was built in 1853 with the new money coming in from the conquest of Algeria—enough to make it the largest church built in France since the Middle Ages, held up by 444 marble columns; adjacent, with less bombast and more charm, stands its Romanesque predecessor, the **Ancienne-Major**. Although the transept was brutally amputated for the new cathedral, note the Ancienne-Major's crossing, a fantasy in brick that sets an octagonal dome on four stepped conical squinches, a typically Provençal conceit. One chapel has a *Descent from the Cross* (early 1500s), a late work from the Della Robbias' Florentine work-shop, and the altar of *SS. Lazarus, Martha, and Mary Magdalene* by Francesco Laurana (1475–81), considered by Anthony Blunt to be 'the earliest purely Italian work on French soil'.

Near the cathedral at the top of Rue du Petit-Puits is a gem of a different cut, the Baroque **Vieille-Charité**, designed by Pierre Puget, a student of Bernini and court architect to Louis XIV—and a native of the Panier. Built by the city fathers between 1671 and 1745 to take in homeless migrants from the countryside, this is one of the world's most palatial workhouses: three storeys of arcaded ambulatories in pale pink stone, overlooking a court with a sumptuous elliptical chapel crowned by an oval dome—a curvaceous Baroque work forced into a straitlaced neo-Corinthian façade in 1863. By 1962, the Charité was in so precarious a state that everyone was evacuated, and in 1985 it reopened as a centre for art, photography and video exhibitions, as well as the Musée d'Archéologie Méditerranéenne.

You could devote the afternoon to the southern side of the Vieux Port. The *filles*, they say, are more discreet here, despite our experience, and

patisserie

especially around the **Opéra**, two blocks south of the Quai des Belges in Place Reyer. Built in 1924, it is graced with a pure Art Deco interior and a fine reputation for Italian opera. Two streets back, in the **Musée Cantini**, 19 Rue Grignan (*© 04 91 54 77 75, open daily 11–6; adm*), holds a massive 20th-century collection of art—by Picabia, Max Ernst, André Masson, Francis Bacon, Balthus, César, Niki de Saint-Phalle, Arman, Ben, and so many more that only a fraction can be displayed at a time. It also displays an exceptional collection of *faïence* made in Marseille and Moustiers, dating back to the 17th century.

On Quai de Rive Neuve, castle walls good enough for Hollywood hide one of the most intriguing Christian sites in Provence, the **Abbaye St-Victor**. St-Victor was founded *c*. AD 416 by Jean Cassien, formerly an anchorite in the Egyptian Thebaid. One account has it that he brought with him from Egypt the mummy of St Victor, though the more popular version says Victor was a Roman legionary who converted to Christianity, and slew at least one sea serpent before being ground to a pulp between a pair of millstones.

The first chapels of the fortified abbey were built into the flank of an ancient stone quarry, and near a Hellenistic necropolis, expanded for

Christian use as a *martyrium* (with rock-cut burial chambers sur-rounding the tomb of a martyr). In the 11th and 12th centuries, when the monks adopted the Rule of St Benedict, they added the church on top, turning the old chapels into crypts and catacombs (*small adm fee*). These are strange and clammy with ancient mystery—the primi-tive bas-reliefs and sarcophagi date from the 3rd century AD, and some of the latter were found to contain seven or eight dead monks crowded like sardines, proof of the popularity of an abbey that founded 300 other monastic houses in Provence and even Sardinia.

Why go to the Riviera when Marseille has one of its very own? From the Vieux Port, you can follow the **Corniche Kennedy**, a dramatic road overlooking a dramatic coast. Amazingly, until the road was built in the 1850s, the first cove, the Anse des Catalans, was so isolated that the Catalan fisherfolk who lived there as squatters in the ruins of the old Lazaretto (the quarantine station) could hardly speak French. This now has the most popular (and the only real) sandy beach. You can walk down to the fishing village of Anse des Auffes ('of the rope-makers'), isolated from the *corniche* until after the Second World War and still determinedly intact. It has a few irresistible restaurants. If you're looking for one recommendation, try delightful Chez Fonfon for dinner.

If you want to get out of town in the afternoon, Sormiou and the more distant *calanques* to the east can be most painlessly reached from Marseille by boat, operating mid-June to mid-September from the Quai des Belges (Groupement des Armateurs Côtiers Marseille, ✆ 04 91 55 50 09).

The wine district of **Cassis** is minute, but was one of the first to be granted AOC status (in 1936). It is considered by the Marseillais to be the only liquid worthy of washing down a *bouillabaisse*, a grilled red mullet, or lobster.

On Cézanne's Tracks

St Sauveur's Cathedral

Artistic, bourgeois, beautiful Aix rings with the sound of music, students and fountains. The darkest plane shadows of Provence cover the Cours Mirabeau, surprisingly for this haughty town named after a count who turned popular hero in the French Revolution. This broad avenue is the manic main street choked with traffic as well as tourists at the café terraces.

The bulk of the old town lies to the north of the Cours Mirabeau. Highlights include the Cathédrale de St-Sauveur and the church of Ste-Marie-Madeleine. South of the Cours Mirabeau, the museum worth a mention is the Musée Granet, which preserves some of the oldest sculptures in France, from Aix's nearby Celto-Ligurian predecessor, Entremont.

But what of the most famous artistic figure to come from Aix, Cézanne? Unfortunately for the town, his contemporary *concitoyens* rejected him and generally despised his work. Something has been done to repair this situation. The French government gave the Musée Granet eight small but representative works in 1984.

To get a pretty unspoilt feel for the countryside which Cézanne would paint with such intensity, head for the Montagne Ste-Victoire. This reduced Table Mountain of Provence became something of an obsession for him. The countryside around it is still extraordinarily calm and unspoilt. The story behind its name is more disturbing. It celebrates the bloody massacre by the Roman general Marius's troops of eastern European tribes that had migrated this far in 102 BC. Cézanne went back time and again to contemplate his mountain. You can spend a good few hours looking at it yourself by going to eat at La Petite Auberge du Tholonet, a surprisingly secretive restaurant with uplifting views onto the mountain.

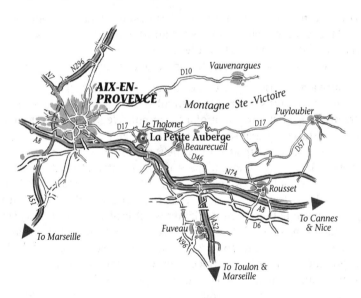

getting there

From Aix, leave the central ring road by the Avenue Ste-Victoire and take the little D17 road, the Route Cézanne, which leads you out of town past a modern Aix fountain that looks like a great watery jelly and along the southern side of the Montagne Ste-Victoire. As you reach the village of Le Tholonet, turn onto the Route de Langesse, the D64E, along which look out for the signs for the *auberge* up on the hillside. If you're coming from the south along the A8 motorway you can avoid going into the centre of Aix, taking the exit before the town, then following the N7 for a short while before turning north for Le Tholonet.

La Petite Auberge du Tholonet

La Petite Auberge du Tholonet, Campagne Régis, Route de Langesse, 13100 Aix-en-Provence, ℭ 04 42 66 84 24, ℗ 04 42 66 91 19. Closed Sun evening and Mon. Menus at 85F, 110F, 135F, 170F and 260F.

This is a restaurant with a view. A splendid artistic one onto the Montagne Ste-Victoire. And it's a country stop where you can find calm after throbbing Aix. La Petite Auberge du Tholonet isn't chic, but slightly (and pleasantly) eccentric and chaotic at first sight.

On arrival you pass a fig tree, then a trough with water splashing into it, the restaurant's *vivier*, although all we could spot was a meagre crayfish. On past a big boot of a flowerpot. We sat down at a table with plastic chairs that sank deeply into the grey gravel and for a few minutes just contemplated Cézanne's great source of inspiration in silence. Below the forbidding mass of the mountain, the village of Le Tholonet is lost in the woods. You can just make out Cézanne's wind-mill right of the church. The restaurant terrace is decorated with geraniums in pots and Chinese lanterns. Little blue paper cloths cover the tables outside, while glasses have been left on their sides and crossed over each other to stop the red napkins blowing away. Shade is provided in part by a striped awning, in part by dried bamboo. You'll want to take a table outside if you possibly can to appreciate the view, but if you're forced inside, the dining room is very light, greenery added by big house plants.

We chose a Provence rosé for the day, a Domaine de la Vallongue from Les Baux, Saignée 95, Réserve C De Clerck. Maybe we were dreamy from the atmosphere, but it tasted to us as though it had hints of strawberries in it. The exclusive La Palette wines are produced in the immediate locality. These red, white, or rosé nectars have been served for the royal fêtes of such diverse monarchs as Good King René and Edward VII, but only two estates still produce these rare fine wines of the south, aged in small casks: the Château Crémade, a 17th-century bastide in Le Tholonet, which bottles magnificent, well-structured red wines and a fruity blanc de blancs; and the celebrated 150-year-old Château Simone, at Meyreuil (off the pretty D 58H), where dark, violet-scented reds are kept for three years in caves carved out by 16th-century Carmelites.

The girl who served us at La Petite Auberge du Tholonet was clearly proud of the place. *'Tout est fait maison, des feuilletés avec l'apéritif aux calissons avec le café,'* she explained—basically, practically everything is home-made. The cooking is well executed Provençal country fare. M. Bonfillon and his son do the bulk of the preparation. Monsieur says that he learnt his profession *'à l'école de cuisine de mon grand-père* (in my grandfather's cookery school)'! His son went to a more formal *école hôtelière*. Although M. Bonfillon trained as an oenologist, cooking runs in the family. One of his grandfather's favourite memories was of the time when he served Edward VII as a boy of only 12—an even earlier forebear of M. Bonfillon had created a restaurant down in Le Tholonet, which was used as a stop for hunters, including British royalty. A plaque in the village commemorates the monarch's visit. La Petite Auberge du Tholonet is a quite recent creation, only opened by M. Bonfillon in 1989. The chefs aim to produce food that is *'très parfumée'* without the herbs being overdone.

If you only have a small appetite you could go for the cheapest menu, the Grande Assiette d'Eté, *spécialités maison, rapide et complet*, with a mix of three tasters for the savoury half and either *faisselle* or a *pâtisserie* of the day for pudding. The 110F menu offers relatively simple choices. The *terrine maison au genièvre, petite salade* was a rich, coarse, tasty pâté with juniper berries, accompanied by a generous salad. Or you could go for a simple tomato and mozzarella salad, or homemade gazpacho. The hors d'oeuvre on the 170F menu offer a little more luxury. The homemade fish soup with very saffrony yellow *rouille* and grated cheese was satisfyingly spicy, served in pleasing earthenware dishes. The generous extra portions offered went down a treat.

Also among the choice of starters on this menu was the excellent olive tart, the recipe reproduced below. The fresh bread is a moreish mixture, with *baguette*, *brioche* and a more rustic variety to try.

Back with the 110F menu, the *poulet fermier grillé sauce Rougail*, a farm chicken dish, was smothered with a hot, tomatoey sauce, ginger giving it a kick. A tomato on the side was stuffed with further herbs and rice. A *compotée* of tomatoes and basil also accompanied the fillet of pink sea bream. The other fish dish, the salmon trout, was supposed to come straight from the restaurant's *vivier*, but it didn't seem to have turned up for our visit. Add cheese and 25F to the 110F menu and you could have a four-course menu at 135F. You could then try the goat's cheese *bouchon*, in the shape of a cork, served on a fig leaf with herbs and olive oil.

With the main courses on the 170F menu you get a better cut of beef (served with a fragrant *garrigues* sauce incorporating two types of olive) and a better type of fish, the sea bass baked in a sea urchin butter sauce. The salmon was accompanied by tarragon butter. *Serpolet* is wild thyme that was used to flavour the rabbit.

The sorbets are made on the premises of course. You might be tempted by the wild strawberry variety. Or for something less sweet, try the *soufflé glacé au marc de Provence*, which is superb, the flavour of the *eau-de-vie* emerging to the full as the pudding melts in your mouth. We couldn't resist the homemade *calissons* the waitress had mentioned, Aix's almond and melon confection, served with coffee.

Tarte aux Olives et Chèvre Chaud

Serves 6

250g/9oz flour
12 tablespoons olive oil
10 tablespoons water
10g/¼ oz fresh yeast
pinch of salt
200g/7oz onions, chopped
500g/1lb 2oz fresh spinach
1 garlic clove, crushed
1 teaspoon fresh thyme
2 eggs
2 tablespoons crème fraîche
200g black olives
6 small round goat's cheeses, halved

Make the pastry in a bowl with the flour, 8 tablesoons of the olive oil, the water, yeast and a pinch of salt. The pastry should be firm and come away from the bowl. Leave to rest for 30 minutes at room temperature.

Meanwhile, fry the onions until golden over a low heat in the remaining olive oil. Then add the spinach, the garlic and thyme and leave to simmer until the liquid has evaporated.

Preheat the oven to 200°C/400°F (gas mark 6).

In a bowl, beat the eggs into the crème fraîche. Add this to the spinach mixture, along with three-quarters of the olives. Roll out the pastry and spread the creamy spinach and olive mixture on top. Bake in the preheated oven for 20 minutes. Sprinkle the rest of the olives over the top, place the goat's cheese halves on top of these and return to the oven for 5–10 minutes.

---

touring around

Elegant and honey-hued, **Aix**, the old capital of Provence, is splashed by a score of fountains, a charming reminder that its very name comes from its waters, *Aquae Sextiae*—sweet waters, mind you, with none of the saltiness of Marseille. For if tumultuous Marseille is the great anti-Paris, Aix-en-Provence is the stalwart anti-Marseille— bourgeois and homogeneous, reactionary and haughtily proud of its aristocratic grandeur and good taste.

Cours Mirabeau, 'the most satisfying street in France', is the centre stage for Aixois society. Laid out in 1649 to replace the south walls, it begins in Place du Général de Gaulle, which takes the old roads from Marseille and Avignon and spins them around the pompous Second Empire fountain La Rotonde. Other fountains punctuate the Cours itself, like the lumpy, mossy Fontaine d'Eau Chaude, oozing up its much esteemed 34°C water, and at the far end, the Fontaine du Roi René, with a fairy-tale statue of the good monarch holding up a bunch of the muscat grapes he introduced to Provence (along with the turkey and the silkworm, which the sculptor left out). Cézanne grew up at 55 Cours Mirabeau, the son of a hatter who later turned banker (on the façade you can still make out the sign of the *chapelier*).

Shops, cafés, and sumptuous, overflowing outdoor markets of every kind fill the narrow lanes and squares of **Vieil Aix**, north of Cours Mirabeau. Enter by way of Rue Espariat from Place Général de Gaulle, and you'll come to a cast-iron Baroque *campanile* and the church of St-Esprit, where a 16th-century retable has portraits of 12 members of the first Provençal *Parlement* cast in the roles of the apostles.

The more orthodox blooms of Aix's flower market lend an intoxi-cating perfume to the square in the very heart of Vieil Aix, in front of the stately Hôtel de Ville (1671), a perfectly proportioned building decorated with stone flowers and fruits and intricate iron grilles. Next to the town hall, the flamboyant Tour de l'Horloge (1510) has clocks telling the hour and the phase of the moon, as well as wooden statues that change with the season.

Rue de Saporta leads north to the **Cathédrale de St-Sauveur**, a curious patchwork of periods and styles that houses a treasure trove of art. The statues that adorned the central flamboyant portal of 1340 were destroyed in the Revolution, except for the Virgin, who was spared when someone popped a red cap of Liberty on her head and made Mary a Marianne. The interior has a central Gothic nave, a Baroque aisle on the left and a Romanesque aisle on the right; on the walls are

26 tapestries illustrating the lives of Christ and the Virgin made in Brussels in 1510. These originally hung in Canterbury Cathedral, but were sold by the Commonwealth, and purchased by a cathedral canon in Paris for next to nothing in 1656.

The cathedral's most famous treasure, Nicolas Froment's Flemish-inspired *Triptyque du Buisson Ardent* (1476), is on the right wall of the Gothic nave, and opened only on request, by the eloquent sacristan (*though usually not on Tues and Sun*). On the two folding panels are portraits of King René, who commissioned the work, and his second wife, kneeling among saints, while the central scene depicts the vision of a monk of St-Victor of Marseille, who saw the Virgin and Child appear in the midst of the miraculous burning bush vouchsafed to Moses. The flames in the green bush symbolize virginity, as does the unicorn; the mirror held by the Child symbolizes his incarnation. The meticulously detailed castles in the background may have been inspired by the towers of Tarascon and Beaucaire on the Rhône.

The Romanesque aisle on the right harbours the oldest section of St-Sauveur, the 5th-century octagonal baptistry, its pool encircled by recycled columns from the temple of Apollo that once stood on this site. Nearby, the 5th-century sarcophagus of St Mitre has a hole that emits an ooze collected by the faithful to heal eye diseases. In the Baroque aisle, the Chapelle de Ste-Anne holds the Renaissance *Altar des Aygosi* (1470), attributed to Francesco Laurana. The *Crucifixion* shows the skull of Adam at the base of the Cross, while above Christ's head is a pelican, which, according to legend, feeds her nestlings with her own blood. Below stand SS. Anne, Marcel, and Marguerite, the latter piously emerging from the shoulders of the dragon that swallowed her whole. Last, but not least, don't miss the light, airy, twin-columned, 12th-century cloister, with capitals daintily carved, though in an awful state of repair.

South of the Cours Mirabeau, and left at the Fountain of the Four Dolphins (unusually equipped with teeth and scales) are the meatier archaeology and art collections of the **Musée Granet** in the former 1675 Priory of the Knights of Malta (*open daily 10–12 and 2–6, closed Tues Sept–May only*). In the basement and ground floor sections there's a superb statue of a Persian Warrior (200 BC) of the Pergamon school, finds from Roman *Aquae Sextiae*, and unique sculptures from the Salian sanctuary at Entremont, believed to be the oldest in Gaul. Appropriately enough for residents of the land that would invent the guillotine, the overall theme is cult decapitation. The remains of 15 embalmed heads were found in the sanctuary, and the sculptures on display here, like death masks, may have been carved to replace real heads that mouldered away. One head, with a hand on top, has the same face as the famous gold mask of Agamemnon from Mycenae (thanks to the proximity of Marseille, Greek stylistic influences were strong).

The Aixois François Granet (1775–1849), after whom the museum is named, was a minor neoclassical artist and a crony of Ingres, enabling him to secure for Aix the latter's enormous *Jupiter and Thetis* (1811), arguably Ingres's most objectionable canvas. Also on display is Ingres's far more palatable and subtle *Portrait of Granet*, painted while the two artists sojourned at Rome's Villa Medici, and canvases by other neoclassical painters including David, Gros, and Granet himself. But what of Cézanne, who took his first drawing-classes in this very building? For years he was represented by only three measly watercolours (no one in Aix would buy his works), until 1984, when the French government rectified the omission by depositing eight small canvases here that touch on the major themes of his work.

Paul Cézanne spent an idyllic childhood roaming Aix's countryside with his best schoolfriend, Emile Zola, and as an adult painted those same landscapes in a way landscapes had never been painted before. Rather than returning to Aix after lunch to see how it remembers its most famous artist son, stay among his landscapes.

The serene, gently rolling countryside around Aix is the quintessence of Provence for those who love Cézanne: the ochre soil, the dusty green cypresses—as still and classical as Van Gogh's are possessed and writhing—the simple geometric forms of its houses and the pyramidal prow of the bluish-limestone Montagne Ste-Victoire.

You can walk around or up the **Montagne Ste-Victoire**. Leave from next to the château in Le Tholonet, with its orange façade set back from the village, for a *circuit* that leads you up to the Barrage Zola, the dam planned by the father of the famous author. Count around two hours for the walk, which takes you through rocks and pines. To climb to the top of the mountain, you need to go a few miles east out of Le Tholonet and find a car park from which you can start. (Alternatively, you can walk up from Les Cabassols on the north side of the mountain, just outside Vauvenargues.) There's a little chapel near the top, and then the cross you'll have noticed from afar, the Croix de Provence. You may find that walks up the mountain may not be permitted in July and August because of the risk of fire. In 1989 a terrible conflagration blackened much of the southern mountainside. Vegetation grew back quickly, but clearly much was lost. For a much less strenuous stroll, go to Le Tholonet's windmill where you should find an art exhibition on in summer.

Or you could continue round the mountain by car. The entire 60km route around it by way of St-Antonin-sur-Bayon, Puyloubier and Pourrières is especially lovely, decked with the vineyards that produce Coteaux d'Aix-en-Provence, relatively recently conferred AOC status.

From Pourrières take the superb gorge north up to Le Puits-de-Rians. Here the vegetation becomes wilder and older, real traditional Provençal forest. At Puits-de-Rians return westwards back to Aix. You'll pass Vauvenargues's oak forest and its famed 14th-century château once owned by Picasso.

Football with Camus in the Southern Lubéron

Silvacane Abbey

On the north side of the Lubéron you have the remains of Peter Mayle's Provence. On the south side you have the remains of one of the greatest writers of the 20th century, Albert Camus. Lourmarin was the last place where he lived and where he and his wife are buried. His ghost wafts around Lourmarin for those interested in his life, although the physical presence that stands out from most angles in the village is the château. Art in the form of painting still thrives in Lourmarin's innumerable galleries.

Several of the places we suggest you visit today aren't dramatically perched on hillsides as the villages on the north side of the Lubéron are, but they are prettily situated. Cadenet looks onto the Durance river, while the austere Abbaye de Silvacane lies just south of Cadenet. The scenery becomes more dramatic as you explore the Pays d'Aigues east of Lourmarin.

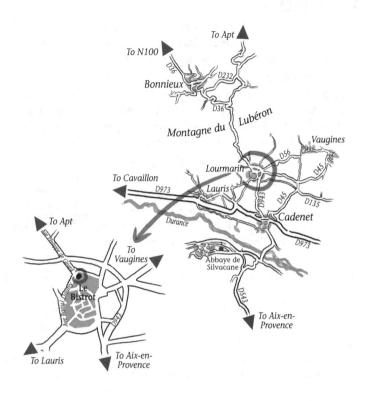

getting there

On the main Michelin map of France, look out for Cadenet, a good way north of Aix, on the D973 east of Cavaillon. Lourmarin lies a short distance north of Cadenet, along the D943. Le Bistrot overlooks the football pitch on the northern side of the village—Camus, an ardent fan of the game and a distinguished goalkeeper in his time, would have approved. It is a heavenly football pitch.

Le Bistrot

Le Bistrot, 2 Avenue Philippe de Girard, 84160 Lourmarin, ☎ 04 90 68 29 74, ✉ 04 90 68 37 44. Closed Thurs. Annual holidays last fortnight Aug and 20 Dec–mid-Jan. Menus at 85F and 115F.

Son of a restaurateur, Jérôme Bulland learnt much of his trade at a great Lyon culinary institution, La Mère Brazier, so it's no surprise that he continues to pay his respects to the Lyonnais, hence the references to *le véritable bouchon lyonnais* and a special, separate Lyonnais menu. He's been settled here for about a decade now.

This is a cheerful, down-to-earth place to eat. In summer the size of the restaurant doubles with its spacious terrace. A table of seasonal vegetables kindly greeted us by the door when we went. Upstairs there's a warm room with large windows overlooking the football pitch, the wall opposite painted ochre and hung with mirrors and a diversity of old posters. We ate outside, under a protective cover that looked like a side awning for a giant caravan.

Come and eat at Le Bistrot on a weekday before 9pm and you can choose the three-course menu for 85F. It starts with one of the most humorous dishes we've seen in Provence, the *ratatouille froide à la menthe, oeuf poché*. This comes in a tall dessert glass and looks like a fruit salad topped with cream. It tastes refreshing too. All the *ratatouille*'s ingredients grow to perfection on the low slopes of the southern Lubéron. You can then choose a Provençal lamb stew in a rich tomato sauce, or the *plat du jour*, followed by a slice of Brie or the pudding of the day.

The more expensive menu is three courses again, with more choices. The *parfait fondant aux foies de volailles, oignons au Porto* is a creamily rich pâté, the melting smoothness contrasting with the sweet bites of onions conserved in Port. Mixed salads are a bit of a speciality here. You might get the chance to try the one given below. Or there might be a very Mediterranean tuna tart, made with the fish, tomatoes, *citron confit* and olive oil.

All the fish and meat dishes come with three vegeta-bles. The *coopérative des fruits et légumes* as well as the more ordinary wine *cave coopérative* lie on a street parallel to the Avenue Philippe de Girard. The choices sound pretty standard, but are well executed. With the beef, we could choose between ceps or Roquefort sauce. The slices of pork came in a mustard sauce, while the salmon was cooked in the trendy manner, on one side only, *à l'unilatéral*. This is the kind of place where you might like to splash out and go *à la carte*. On the Provençal carte, look out for the house *bouillabaisse de morue* or *gambas* panfried *à la Provençale*.

Many of your stock French puddings are on the menu: *île flottante*, profiteroles, *gâteau fondant au chocolat*... The apple puddings are the most interesting, the *terrine aux pommes Kevin* (what a title!) containing caramelized apples flavoured with Grand Marnier and vanilla, served with whipped cream and *crème anglaise*.

Panaché de Salades aux Poivrons et Calamars Grillés

Serves 4

1 frisée lettuce or endive

4 prepared squid

2 large red peppers

200ml/7fl oz olive oil

3 garlic cloves, chopped

handful fresh parsley, chopped

salt

100ml/4fl oz sherry or white wine vinegar

1 heaped teaspoon mustard

pinch of curry powder

1 large carrot, peeled and cut into batons

1 apple (Golden Delicious or Granny Smith), peeled, cored and cut into batons

Separate and wash the salad leaves, choosing the yellow crunchy ones, then trim and drain them.

Rub the skin off the squid under running water, dry them, then cut across into 1cm/½in-wide strips to make rings. Wash the peppers and slice them like the squid. Add the squid to a very hot pan containing half the olive oil. Add the peppers, reduce the heat a little and cook until the liquid rendered by the squid has completely evaporated, then sauté to brown them. Add the garlic and parsley. Sauté over a high heat until cooked and salt generously at the end.

Shake the remaining olive oil, vinegar, mustard and curry powder together in a clean screw-topped jar and drizzle over the salad leaves. Toss to coat them evenly with the dressing. Place the salad in heaps on 4 plates, and sprinkle the carrot and apple batons evenly over each serving of salad. Scoop the squid and peppers out of the pan with a slotted spoon and scatter over each of the salads. Serve immediately.

touring around

In the morning go and have a look round **Cadenet**, an ancient place overlooking the rocky bed of the Durance. It began as a pre-Celtic *oppidum*; even older are some of the cave dwellings that can be seen in the cliffs behind the village. Other caves served as refuges for persecuted Waldensian Protestants in the 1500s. In 1540, the *Parlement* of Aix oversaw the burning of 19 Waldensian villages in the Lubéron, including Lourmarin. Have a peek inside the parish church, St-Etienne, on the northern edge of town. The baptismal font has well-preserved reliefs of a Bacchic orgy; scholars reckon it to be 3rd-century, but disagree over whether it was originally a sarcophagus or a bathtub.

Cross the Durance for the sobering **Abbaye de Silvacane** (*open daily exc Tues, 9–12 and 2–5; adm*). Life as a medieval Cistercian was no picnic. Besides the strict discipline and a curious prejudice against heating, there was always the chance the Order might send you to somewhere in the middle of a swamp. They built this, the first of the 'Three Sisters of Provence', in just such a location because they meant to reclaim it. The very name, *silva cana*, or forest of rushes, is a reminder of their efforts. They took a century or two, but they did the job, as you can see today from the fertile farmlands around Silvacane. A Benedictine community had already been established here when the Cistercians arrived in 1147. Work began on the present buildings soon after, partially financed by the barons of Les Baux, and Silvacane became quite prosperous. Bad frosts in the 1300s killed all the olives and vines, starting Silvacane on its long decline. When the government bought the complex to restore it in 1949, it was being used as a barn. The church is as chastely fair as its younger sisters at Sénanque and Thoronet, though perhaps more austere and uncompromising; even the apse is a plain rectangle.

The obvious attraction in **Lourmarin**, at a slightly haughty distance from the rest of the village, is the château (*open for guided tours except Tues, closed Nov–Mar; adm*). Well restored, it's now the property of the Académie of Aix, which uses it for cultural programmes, concerts and exhibitions, so look out for what's on when you're there.

Before or after lunch, have a wander round the village itself. Lourmarin may not look pretentious at first sight, but on closer inspection it does have an extraordinary number of art galleries and hairdressers' in it, which suggests an extremely glamorous side. Some of the hairdressers' seem to serve as art galleries at the same time...or maybe it's the other way round. If all these salons leave your head reeling, you could pause at one of the many cafés also crammed into what is basically a very small but very busy village.

You can then walk a short distance out of the village along a curving plane-lined road leading to the cemetery. Be particularly mindful of traffic as Camus died in a car crash; the manuscript for his last unfinished novel, *Le Premier Homme,* which he had with him when he died, has only very recently been published and translated. Touchingly, rosemary was flourishing on Albert's tomb, various mementoes left by visitors scattered upon it. His wife Françoise's grave was fragrant with lavender. It was a moving moment to stand in front of his tomb among the packed graves in this neat-walled cemetery, the distinctive dark cypresses marking the resting place of the dead. Camus isn't the only well-known French author buried here. Henri Bosco may not cut the mustard on the international scene, but he is very widely known in France, in particular for his children's books.

You might like to head out into the **Lubéron** countryside in the afternoon. Like many parts of rural Provence, the Lubéron presents a puzzling contrast—how its villages became such eminently civilized places, set amidst a landscape (and a population) that is more than a little rough around the edges. The real Lubéron is a land of hunters stalking wild boar over Appalachian-like ridges, and weatherbeaten farmers in ancient Renaults full of rabbit cages and power tools. There are other regions of Provence, equally scenic and rustic, that merit being frozen into a nature preserve, but the Lubéron was the one most in danger of being destroyed by a rash of outsiders and unplanned holiday villas. The Parc Régional du Lubéron was founded in 1977, a cooperative arrangement between the towns and villages that covers most of the territory between Manosque and Cavaillon; quite a few (often where the mayor is an estate agent or a notary) have decided not to participate at all. The Lubéron is not an exceptional nature area like the Mercantour. Still, the Park is doing God's work, protecting rare species like the long-legged Bonelli's eagle, a symbol of the Midi that needs plenty of room to roam and is nearing extinction.

Head east from Lourmarin for the southern end of the park, its sleepiest corner, with pretty villages below the Lubéron's southern slopes. The D56 takes you to lovely little Vaugines. The next village, **Cucuron**, has a wider claim to fame, no longer simply for its melons and olive oil, but now also thanks to the part it played in the recent film *Le Hussard sur le toit* (The Horseman on the Roof), an adaptation of a work by Provençal and nature writer Jean Giono. From Cucuron you could continue along the southern slopes of the Lubéron via Cabrière d'Aigues, La Motte d'Aigues and Peypin d'Aigues to La Bastide-des-Jourdans.

Or head to **Ansouis** from Cucuron. Ansouis is a *village perché* built around the sumptuously furnished Château de Sabran (*open daily, exc Tues in winter, 2.30–6*), still in the hands of the original family: a Henry IV monumental stair leads to Flemish tapestries, Italian Renaissance furniture, portraits and later Bourbon bric-a-brac. The atmosphere is wonderfully snooty, but they let us in to visit just the same. For an airier, pleasanter castle without the bric-a-brac, try La Tour d'Aigues, just to the east.

A Sado-Masochistic Chain of Villages in the Northern Lubéron

Bonnieux

The Marquis de Sade was followed by Peter Mayle, two writers to go down in Provençal history as *enfants terribles* of the Lubéron. The wacky, or more like whacking, aristocrat had his great family pile on the melodramatic hilltop of Lacoste over-looking much of the northern Lubéron. The former ad man's house was a little more discreet, by Ménerbes. The success of his slicky entertaining portrayal of the area apparently drove him out, to the quiet of California.

Their two villages count among the plethora of splendid hill-side hamlets dotted around the northern Lubéron. To be fair to Peter Mayle, the area became a favourite holiday retreat for wealthy city dwellers well before he wrote about it. Bonnieux, clinging to the north side of the Lubéron and visible for miles and miles around, occupies an excellent central position for exploring the villages of the region: to the west lie Lacoste, Ménerbes and Oppède-le-Vieux; to the north, Gordes, Roussillon and St-Saturnin, to name a few. Just north of

Gordes, the Abbaye de Sénanque proves rather more spiritual, a deeply serious and dry Cistercian foundation in a barren valley, suddenly and uncharacteristically brightened for one brief patch of the year by lavender rows in flower.

getting there

Bonnieux lies a little south of the N100 that links Avignon and Cavaillon to the west with Apt to the east. Approaching from the north, from many angles you can see the village stuck to the northern slopes of the Montagne du Lubéron. Beginning the climb into the old centre, try to park on the Place Gambetta. From here it's just a short walk up to the Place Carnot with both the restaurant and the *office de tourisme*.

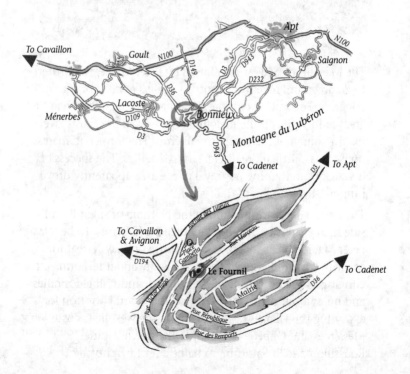

A Sado-Masochistic Chain of Villages in the Northern Lubéron

Le Fournil

Le Fournil, 5 Place Carnot, 84480 Bonnieux, ✆ 04 90 75 83 62, ✉ 04 90 75 96 19. Closed Mon all day and Tues lunch, except July and Aug, when closed Mon all day and Sat lunch; also 20 Nov–10 Dec and 5 Jan–5 Feb. Menus at 90F, 118F and 165F.

Le Fournil pretty well has it all. A wonderful Provençal square with splashing fountain and faded old shop signs. A couple of atmospheric troglodyte dining rooms built into the hillside just in case it should rain in summer and which are cosily warm for winter. And a gay feel to it. Actually gay in both senses of the word. The place is run by Guy Malbec and Jean Christophe Lèche, a couple with long experience in some of the best French establishments. They make no bones about their relationship and AIDS is clearly on the agenda here—a little basket full of red ribbons lies by the entrance, cards on befriending the HIV positive at the troglodyte loo's wash basin.

Jean Christophe Lèche runs the *service* and Guy Malbec does the cooking. Some of the waiters suffer from a bit of gay attitude, some are warm and friendly. When we went, the season's outfit was black trousers and grey T-shirts. The tablemats were, unsurprisingly, pink.

The Château La Canorgue Côtes-du-Lubéron is a more subdued lovely peachy pink colour. The estate produces good wine from vineyards set around a beautiful 16th-century château by Bonnieux (Route du Pont-Julien, ✆ 04 90 75 81 01). The vineyards that produce AOC Côtes-du-Lubéron actually stretch across a wide area between the mountains of the lower Durance and the Calavon valley around Apt.

On a hot summer day, the *gâteau de tomates frais aux herbes et tapenade* makes a deliciously refreshing starter, the diced tomatoes chilled in a light jelly, plenty of basil adding flavour to this pretty red 'cake'. The ever-so-slightly bitter taste of the *tapenade* is an extremely good contrast. The shrimps with marinated courgettes come on a bed of beansprouts, again the mixture of textures as satisfying as the mixture of tastes. Cavaillon melon with shavings of raw ham might sound a bit hackneyed, but you should know that melons are the main claim to fame of the town of Cavaillon, at the western end of the Lubéron. The three starters mentioned were the options on the 118F menu. On the more elaborate 165F menu you could choose between stuffed squid, a chilled tomato soup with an anchovy cream and little toasts covered in *poutargue*, and the vegetable tart with fresh goat's cheese.

Back with the 118F menu, and on to the main courses. The *mignon de porc à la sauge* was extremely tender, a sign of good pork, and slightly salty, served with garlic *en chemise*. Sweet vinegar sauce set off the duck *magret*. These dishes were accompanied by thin slices of potatoes and slender *batons* of courgettes. The tuna steak came with *tabbouleh* and a light tarragon *sabayon*, the roast chicken with tangy *citrons confits*. On the more expensive menu, the choices were between roast lamb served with a coconut and chive purée and a *picatta de veau aux aubergines*, the escalope very finely cut and prepared with parmesan and balsamic vinegar as well as the aubergines, while the monkfish was flavoured with fennel and accompanied by *tomates confites*. You could also have goat's cheese as an extra course with the more expensive option.

The puddings make a fitting end to the meal, as light as the other dishes. You could go for the old-fashioned plum tart. Or the *gâteau tiède de chocolat*, which was really like a warm, rich, chocolate brownie on a tart base, or a blancmange ('white eat' in French) made with delicious almond milk. *A la carte*, you might also be tempted by a *galette de figues, jus au Porto* or the *pain perdu avec confiture de vieux garçons*, bread and butter pudding with a jam made from mixed fruits. The reference to a *vieux garçon* seemed like a rather in gay joke, it being the French expression for a bachelor, although in times past bachelors were apparently sometimes stereotyped as rather mean or eccentric, and the image conjured up might be of an old codger going round collecting all the fallen fruit in his garden to then cook it up together.

We did feel in seventh heaven at Le Fournil. We ordered extra glasses of wine and tried deciphering the old signs on the shop fronts opposite. There were worn words advertising a hatter's, hunting equipment, a tobacconist's, a haberdasher's. We craned our necks up to the imposing sheer wall of rock behind the restaurant leading precipitously to ramparts high above us. And then we simply let ourselves be happily hypnotized by the sound of the water splashing in the fountain.

Morue Fraîche Poêlée, Pomme de Terre Ecrasée, Jus de Cébette

Serves 4

1kg/2lbs 4oz potatoes
coarse sea salt
1.5kg/3lbs 5oz fresh cod
1 cébette (new onion) or 2 shallots
250ml/8fl oz chicken stock
25g/1oz butter, diced
1 bunch chives, chopped
150ml/¼ pint olive oil, plus 3 tablespoons

Preheat the oven to 180°C/350°F (gas mark 4).

Bake the potatoes in the preheated oven, laying them on a baking tray or in a roasting tin in which you have scattered coarse sea salt. Leave to cook until tender (about 35 minutes).

Cut the cod into 8 steaks of about 170g/6oz.

Chop the cebétte or shallots and place it in a saucepan with the chicken stock. Cook until the liquid has reduced by two-thirds. Whisk in the butter until melted and amalgamated, then keep to one side.

Take the potatoes out of the oven and peel them. Mash them with a fork. Chop the chives and mix with the mash. Slowly add the 150ml/¼ pint of olive oil.

Sauté the cod steaks in batches in a non-stick pan using 1 tablespoon of the remaining olive oil, adding more as required. Serve immediately.

touring around

Ultra-pretty, ultra-pricey **Gordes** is the village in the northern Lubéron with the most obvious attractions around it. If you want to go to the Abbaye de Sénanque, the *bories*, or the Vasarély museum, we'd suggest you try to arrive early in the morning in high season. Otherwise, you're likely to end up in the tourist crush. The first thing you'll notice about the striking *village perché* is that it has a rock problem. They have it under control; the vast surplus has been put to use in houses and sheds, and also for the hundreds of thick stone walls that make Gordes seem more like a southern Italian village than one in Provence. The stones made agriculture a bad bet here, so the Gordiens planted olives instead, and became famous for them—at least until the terrible frost of 1976 killed off most of the trees.

Hungarians are renowned for their cleverness; they say a man from Budapest can enter a revolving door behind you and come out in front. The late Victor Vasarély, a poster artist, arrived in France from Budapest in 1929; he always had his mind set on something a little more serious, and the abstract madness of the post-war era finally gave him a chance. With a modicum of talent and a tidal wave of verbal mystification about the 'plastic alphabet' and 'escaping the ephemerality' of figurative art, Vasarély became an op-art celebrity in the '60s. Few artists have ever managed to commandeer a castle as a personal monument; he convinced Gordes to allow it by paying for the restorations. Hence the Vasarély Didactic Museum (*open daily exc Tues, 10–12 and 2–6; adm*). Early attempts at drawing are mostly self-portraits; the later works that made him famous are all tidy and colourful.

Gordes was a fierce resistance stronghold in the war and suffered for it, with wholesale massacres of citizens and the destruction of much of the village. The damage the Nazis did has been redeemed; the village centre, all steep, cobbled streets and arches, is extremely attractive.

The **Abbaye de Sénanque**, the loveliest of the Cistercian Three Sisters of Provence, lies 4km north of Gordes on the D177. The church may be almost a double of the one at Thoronet, but built in the warm golden stone of the Vaucluse and set among lavender fields and oak groves, it makes quite an impression. The church (*open daily 10–12* *and 2–6; adm*), begun about 1160, shows the same early Cistercian seriousness as Thoronet and Silvacane, and has been changed little over the centuries; even the original altar is present. Most of the monastic buildings have also survived, including a lovely cloister, the *chauffoir*, the only heated room, where the monks transcribed books, and a refectory with displays giving a fascinating introduction to Sénanque and the Cistercians.

Across the Midi they are called *bories*, or *garriotes*, or *capitelles*, or a dozen other local names. In Provence there are some 3000 of them, but the largest collection in one place is the **Village des Bories** just south of Gordes, off the D2. A *borie* is a small dry-stone hut, usually with a well-made corbelled dome or vault for a ceiling. From their resemblance to Neolithic works they have always intrigued scholars. Recently it has been established, however, that though the method of building goes way back, none of the *bories* you see today is older than the 1600s. This group of 12 *bories* has been restored as a rural museum (*open daily 9–8 summer, 9–5.30 winter; adm*).

East of Gordes, some of the land has sandy deposits deeply coloured by iron oxides or ochre, the material used in prehistoric times as skin-paint, and later to colour everything from soap to rugs. Centuries of mining have left some bizarre landscapes—cliffs and pits and peaks in what the locals claim are '17 shades of red'—there are also deep yellows and creams and occasional other hues besides. **Roussillon**, the Ruddy One, has the most spectacular ochre landscapes and richly coloured, very sought-after and expensive houses. It also occupies a spectacular hilltop site, and well it should, as centuries of mining have removed nearly everything for miles around. Bilingual playwright and Nobel prize winner for literature Samuel Beckett spent the war years exiled in Roussillon; the rural peace and quiet at that time gave him a nervous breakdown. Apt, which lies to the east, claims to be the 'World Capital of Candied Fruits', *fruits confits*. Not the most attractive of towns, it does have an excellent Saturday market and the Maison du Pays du Lubéron, the main information centre of the Lubéron Regional Park. South of Roussillon, near the meeting point of the N100 and the D149 (south of the N100), cross the well-preserved Roman bridge, the Pont Julien, to take you to Bonnieux for lunch.

After lunch, the walk around **Bonnieux** can be slightly taxing, as the paths to the top of the village are steep and winding. Mind you, you don't need to climb very high to get fabulous views over the fertile valley to the north, leading to the hills of the plateau de Vaucluse. Climbing slowly up through the village you pass by the grand door-ways and little courtyards of the substantial village houses. At the top of the village, the views extend for miles and miles, cut up in parts by wide-spreading cedar branches. Take the lower 19th-century steeple down below for your bearings, and to the left of it you should be able to spot the villages of Roussillon, Gordes and Lacoste. The public garden around the run-down, rarely open church at the top of Bonnieux is surprisingly tatty, with a rusty Christ standing out among the scrubby vegetation. Back down below in the village, you may spot a third belfry, part of a 17th-century priory turned into the charming Hostellerie du Prieuré hotel.

Leave Bonnieux for the Marquis de Sade's village, a few kilometres west along the D109. **Lacoste** is a trendy *village perché*; overlooking the village is a gloomy ruined castle, the former home of no less a menace than the Marquis de Sade (d. 1814). The French are a bit embarrassed about the author of *120 Journées de Sodome*, but he certainly wasn't insane, and he is a literary figure of some note, taking to extremes the urge for self-expression that came with the dawn of the Romantic movement. Oddly enough, the Marquis seems to have been a descendant of Petrarch's Laura. The thought of it obsessed him for life, and he saw her in visions in the castle here. The castle, burned in the Revolution, is currently undergoing a slow restoration by the local *commune*.

Continuing along the D109, you come to **Ménerbes**, honey-coloured, artsy and cuter than cute (with an attitude to match). Ménerbes is so narrow, from some angles it looks like a ship, cruising out of the Lubéron towards Avignon; at the top is a small square, about 6m across, with balconies on either side. The D188 road continues west almost to the top of the Petit Lubéron, and **Oppède-le-Vieux**, with its ruined castle, which can be explored, but watch your step. Perhaps it has a curse on it; this was the home of the bloodthirsty Baron d'Oppède, leader of the genocide here against the Waldensian Protestants in the 1540s.

Ringing Rocks of the Montagne de Lure

the old citadel Forcalquier

East of the Mont Ventoux lies its relatively ignored northern Provençal twin. The Montagne de Lure is bald-headed too. Clambering up on top of its giant's pate you get amazing views all around on a clear day. As well as admiring the Alps, you can also look down clearly on to the flat valley of the Durance running through the centre of the *département* of the Alpes-de-Haute-Provence. The next four chapters feature areas from this much less well-known part of Provence, the Provence of the great nature writer Jean Giono. The land and the villages are generally more barren, less groomed here.

One splendid exception is the hilltop Simiane-la-Rotonde, southwest of Lardiers where we eat. Simiane counts among the most beautiful villages in Provence, superbly done up by its wealthy new inhabitants. Simiane onions, elongated, mauve and extremely tasty, can be found in markets across Provence. The name of the village of Banon between Lardiers and Simiane is indissociably linked with a fine sheep's cheese.

By contrast with Simiane, south of Lardiers, the town of Forcalquier is a bit of a scruff, but it also has a quite lovable character.

getting there

Lardiers is a very small, charmingly plain village near the foot of the Montagne de Lure. On the main Michelin map of France seek out St-Etienne-lès-Orgues north of Forcalquier. Where the D950 between Forcalquier and Banon meets the D951, 7km west of St-Etienne, turn up the small road to the village. Approached along a dry, flat valley, Lardiers itself is a dry village lost up a very quiet road. The latter was so deserted when we took it that we encountered a snake slithering nonchalantly and wearily along, as though the road were made for it. You can't get lost once you arrive in Lardiers. You can park in front of the village *lavoir* on the little square on which the café-restaurant stands, close to one of the smallest *mairies* ever seen.

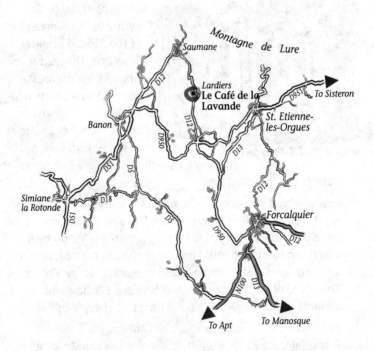

Café-Restaurant de la Lavande

Café-Restaurant de la Lavande, 04230 Lardiers, ℗ 04 92 73 31 52. Closed Mon, Jan and possibly one week in Nov. Menu at 85F.

Nothing seems to stir on certain days in Lardiers. Just one small family sat at the couple of simple tables outside the *bistrot* when we arrived. With its brick-arched windows, this is not a grand place, more like a basic village bar with a restaurant in the same room. It's small, clean, and interesting.

The bar-cum-restaurant also serves as a tiny local grocery. On the shelves is a selection of wines, beans, summer truffles, Camargue rice... Next to them stands the typical French bar counter, a row of high chairs drawn up close to it. You can't miss the trophies on the shelves behind. The odd horse picture, horse plate and horse sculpture hint at a particular passion of Norbert, the man behind the bar.

In the trapezoid room we sat next to the small fireplace cluttered with cookery books: *50 Recettes de pain, La Nostalgie est derrière le comptoir* (Nostalgia is Behind the Counter), *La Cuisine d'Algérie*. Although Lardiers may seem miles and miles from even a minor town, quiet, detached and unmodernized, the chef, Emmanuelle Burollet, is certainly not inward-looking. She describes her cuisine as Mediterranean, but influenced by many of its shores. Spanish, North African, or Greek touches might spring up among the Provençal. Born in Libya, Emmanuelle's parents lived in Tunisia for a long time before returning to France. The dishes in which the food is presented may be Spanish or North African.

Everyone in Emmanuelle's family cooks, the men as well as the women. Actually the family originates from the Bordelais, in western France, but they always came here for holidays. Her sister opened a restaurant in Forcalquier, in 1982, and Emmanuelle opened this *bistrot* with Norbert in July 1995. She does family-style cooking, hearty, flavoursome, generous. That said, as at the family table, you can't choose what you eat, so best check when you book or on the day what is likely to be served.

Emmanuelle's moustachioed partner can advise you on the wine to drink with the meal. Cairanne from the same area as Gigondas is clearly a particular favourite, the estates chosen with great care. The rare, more local wine isn't to be dismissed. The Domaine de La Blaque is from the little-known wine *appellation* of Coteaux de Pierrevert. It's very pleasant and light, to be drunk fresh and young. The other subject Norbert will speak passionately about is English thorough-breds. He owns some himself and follows racing very closely.

Meanwhile Emmanuelle must be manically busy in the kitchen. The array of hors d'oeuvre is always substantial, with many vegetable dishes. These hors d'oeuvre are the Café de la Lavande's answer to tapas. You don't choose; Emmanuelle brings out a row of brown pottery dishes full of tempting things. Don't be overwhelmed—many of these preparations turn out to be surprisingly light. 'People moan if the *brandade de morue* isn't on the menu,' she responds to our enthusiastic first tasting. This is an utterly delicious example of the popular Provençal dish. It consists of mashed salt cod, with olive oil and milk whisked in, and a touch of garlic added. Beneath the crusty top, as you taste the mix below it begins to melt and then takes on a slightly more chewy, satisfying texture, leaving a very pleasantly lingering flavour in the mouth. The red peppers were melting too, served with olives and anchovies, giving a mix of sweetness and saltiness. The couple sometimes go as far as Collioures, on the French border with the Catalan side of Spain, to seek out the best anchovies. The tender potatoes could well come from as far west as Noirmoutier, an island off the French Atlantic coast, from which Emmanuelle and Norbert also buy fine salt.

The *principe de base* here is *bons produits*, as you can taste—the couple really care about getting good produce to reach this isolated village. On the day we went, the hors d'oeuvre dishes also included little artichokes flavoured with cloves and coriander, served in plenty of oil, the latter needed in order to tenderize them a bit, and pumpkin cooked to such a tenderness that you could easily eat the rind.

On first seeing the array of starters we felt we would never have room for a main course, let alone pudding. But in fact we finished off virtually every hors d'oeuvre dish and didn't feel particularly bloated. If you have a small appetite, taste just a little of each dish and save room for the other courses. The *plat principal* we had was very tender white rabbit in quite a light sauce. Most intriguing of all was the vegetable accompaniment, translucent yellow shreds of a noodle or thin pasta-like vegetable seasoned with plenty of pepper. It turned out to be spaghetti marrow, nicely crunchy. In summer Emmanuelle often likes to prepare stuffed vegetables of different kinds for the main course, for example, peppers, tomatoes, courgettes, or even onions.

The puddings are no less copious than the rest. You're presented with a choice of three on the plate: in our case, we were treated, or maybe challenged, to a piece of red plum tart, a light raspberry and cream sponge, and a slice of chocolate cake. But that wasn't quite all—alongside these, Emmanuelle had plonked down a big decorative Moroccan dish, full of pears in mulled wine with large slices of lemon, flavoured with cloves and nutmeg. We were just left to help ourselves in case we were still hungry.

Replete, we couldn't be bothered to stir as a little grey Egyptian-looking kitten rushed in to do battle with a wayward hornet, which it seemed to have mistaken for an amusing toy. It was surprising to see so much sprightliness in the village, especially after such a satisfyingly and soporifically filling country lunch.

Tarte au Potiron (ou Courge)

Serves 6

For the pastry:
250g/9oz flour
120g/4 ½oz butter
pinch of salt
100ml/4fl oz water or beer

For the filling:

¼ medium-sized ripe pumpkin or marrow

25g/1oz butter

120g/4½oz nuts, chopped

100g/4oz raisins

3 tablespoons honey

3 eggs, lightly beaten

First, make the shortcrust pastry. Mix the flour with the butter and a pinch of salt. Slowly add and mix in enough of the water or beer to form a dough. Knead the pastry well, then set aside for at least 1 hour. Preheat the oven to 180°C/350°F (gas mark 4).

Peel the pumpkin or marrow, cut it into pieces, then cook it very gently over a low heat with the butter, stirring regularly. When it is cooked, mash it with a fork to make a purée. Add the nuts, raisins and honey, followed by the eggs.

Roll out the shortcrust pastry very thinly and use it to line a 20cm/8in tart tin. Fill with the pumpkin or marrow mixture and bake in the preheated oven for approximately 30 minutes.

---

touring around

We suggest a little touring in three directions from Lardiers, but easily feasible in a day. It doesn't matter in which order you try the suggestions. All three places are generally quiet, sometimes magically so.

You might come to Lardiers from the Mont Ventoux to the east rather than from the Durance valley. In that case, head across the barren, lavender-brushed Plateau d'Albion to **Simiane-la-Rotonde** in the morning. Simiane is topped by a keep-like structure that looks like a sand castle. This is the Rotonde which is included in the village name. You could park near it. Romanesque and Gothic features emerge in the courtyard by which you can enter this weird stocky tower. Inside, the cupolas and carved Romanesque heads stuck in unusual positions make it doubly curious. Apparently it served as the lords' chapel.

From here climb down the steep and slippery cobbled streets to explore the village. Simple ceramic plaques give directions to the things you can go and see. Simiane is small, but a slightly confusing maze. Wild flowers grow, carefully tended, on the sides of the narrow streets. A good many of the doors and doorways are remarkable; look out for instance for the scrolled bat face over the door of the Maiso Pellissier des Granges. There are innumerable delightful little surprises in the buildings and the decoration of the village, an ornamental piece of stone sculpting here, some herringbone patterning in a construction there, the odd modern statue popping up here and there.

We stopped at the covered market place, a beautiful construction held up by three basic stone columns and from which you get gentle views down onto the wide valley below, with scarcely a modern house in sight to mar the medieval look. The day we were there, the only note to disturb the calm came from the dogs barking at each other in the valley. The village cats remained impervious. House martens twisted and flitted around in the air. This covered market was set out with the plastic chairs and tables of the Café-Restaurant La Rotonde. Most likely you'll be so seduced by this village that if you get a chance you'll return. You should then come and try this lovely restaurant.

Between Simiane and Lardiers stop briefly at **Banon**. If you come on a Tuesday morning, you may want to linger longer for the market. On that day you'll be able to appreciate to the full the ewe's cheese Banon is famous for. The old fortified village is attractive. Look out for the luxurious 16th-century *pigeonniers*.

After lunch, you might like to take a walk around the village of **Lardiers** or in Lardiers's valley. The village church has preserved a Romanesque doorway with some beautiful foliage capitals. For a much more strenuous walk to work off the meal, it's four or five kilometers to the great old oak, described as the *chêne millénaire*, one thousand years old. Ask the way. It needs four or five people to join arms to be able to circle the oak's circumference.

We preferred to climb the **Montagne de Lure** by car. You can tell this mountain is nowhere near as popular a tourist site as the Mont Ventoux by the road up to it. At some points it is so bad it starts to make you think of what travel must have felt like in the time of the horse and carriage. You don't get the same diversity of views as when you're climbing up the side of the Mont Ventoux. Here you go pretty well straight north up the mountain. Low down, you pass through pines the colour of olive trees. As you climb higher you leave a posse of chalets and a ski lift behind you. On the calm day we went, we only met two cars.

At the top, extraordinary slices of friable rocks lie around in great piles, as though delicately built up by hand. They look so fragile, as though they ought to fall in a strong wind and slip away into the steep and beautifully desolate valley of Jabron to the north. Beyond and to the east, the Alps were spectacular, the few peaks that had snow looking much closer than from the Mont Ventoux, itself visible to the west.

We went for a walk by ourselves near the summit. No tourist stalls, no tourist buses as on the Mont Ventoux. A sign near the radio masts warned '*attention troupeaux*', but we didn't see any sheep or goats or shepherds up here. We just heard the wind whistling gently, the odd bird singing, and as we picked up some of the stones and knocked them together, ringing rocks.

Our descent from the mountain was slowed by a herd of fat sheep, however. We went on to **Forcalquier**. Early evening is a good time to arrive in this town crowned by Christianity, in the form of a neo-Romanesque octagon of a building with a dome on top. After a steep climb, sour-faced *modillons* look out sulkily over you from this building, angels play music on its roof, while the dome is topped, in typical 19th-century taste, by a statue of the Virgin. The place pays homage to Pope Urban II, '*lou Papo de la Crousado que vengué benesi Fourcauquié*' the French pope who came here on his inspiring tour to whip up support for the First Crusade at the end of the 11th century.

In the atmospheric old town, the narrow streets are much scruffier than in more touristy Provence, which makes for rather a nice change if you're sick of too much overprettification. The former Cathédrale Notre-Dame lies on the edge of the tightly packed *vieille ville*, an imposing mix of Romanesque and Gothic. On the generous square beyond you'll find a string of cafés, the sturdily charming looking Hostellerie des Deux Lions, a 17th-century coaching inn which prepares solid Provençal cooking, and a Baroque church that has been irreverently converted into a cinema!

Refinement Along the Durance Valley

Le Vieux Colombier, our restaurant choice along the Durance valley, lies between the major towns of the Alpes-de-Haute-Provence, Manosque on the Durance, and Digne down the Bléone. Opposite it, on the protected heights over-looking the river, medieval monks built a string of beautiful monasteries and churches. Hilltop Lurs, Ganagobie and St-Donat sit relatively close together.

Le Vieux Colombier

Manosque and Digne aren't generally considered tourist destinations, but both have a few small attractions. Manosque was home to the Provençal writer par excellence, Jean Giono. Thermal Digne became the retreat of the extraordinary Frenchwoman Alexandra David-Neel, deeply influenced by Buddhism and Tibet, who lived until 1969 and the ripe old age of 101. The geological park around Digne can reveal traces of much older indigenous elements, not just special rock formations, but also ancient fossils, including that of an ichthyosaurus, a prehistoric fish.

The Durance was traditionally maligned as one of the three plagues of Provence, along with the *mistral* and the *parlement* at Aix. The Durance's flash flooding may be more under control these days, but the valley has become rather a busy thoroughfare. To discover an isolated valley off it, undisturbed by modern advances, you could take a trip up the picturesque valley of the Asse.

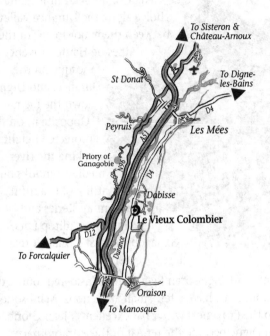

getting there

Halfway down the Durance as it crosses through the Alpes-de-Haute-Provence, Dabisse lies on the orchard-lined D4, on the opposite side of the valley from the A51 motorway and the monastery of Ganagobie, midway between Les Mées and Oraison. The restaurant Le Vieux Colombier is about one km south of Dabisse, set close to the road. Look out for the signs and the sturdy farm building by itself on the eastern side, with a large private car park provided off the highway.

Le Vieux Colombier

Le Vieux Colombier, 04190 Dabisse, Les Mées, ✆ 04 92 34 32 32, 🖷 04 92 34 34 26. Closed Wed and Sun evening, and first week in Jan. Menus from 95F, plus ones at 210F and 295F.

The road to Le Vieux Colombier, a square-shouldered farm built in 1835, is lined with thickly planted fruit orchards; you may see the trees covered in their 'hair nets', presumably there to protect them from the birds. Signs along the way point you down tracks to various farms selling homegrown fruits and honey.

Sylvain and Marie Nowak look too young to have been established here since the early 1990s. They restored the farm which is now their home and restaurant, crowned by the outstanding feature after which it is named, the *colombier*, a dovecote or pigeon-loft. Marie, petite, anxious to please, comes from a *pied noir* family, formerly living in North Africa. Sylvain, *petit*, in his chef's whites, is very relaxed, with a beaming smile. From the Ariège, he has cooked his way round France and also done a stint in Arabia.

You eat in what they believe was once the *bergerie*, or home to sheep and goats. Massive rounded beams hold up the ceiling. Big pale pink-to-beige tiles keep in line with the rustic feel. The dining room is spacious, with around a dozen tables set inside. A plant box in the centre helps to lighten the evident bulk of the room. Local paintings decorate some of the walls.

Outside in the garden, the setting is more modern. A bright-blue-bottomed pool is surrounded by crazy paving. From out here you can look back onto the pebbly façade of the farm, its grey shutters divided up by three cypresses planted as columns right against the wall. You get a good view of the pigeon-loft from here. In the simple back garden, figs, quinces, cherries and herbs grow along with roses and dahlias.

Care is paid to every culinary detail. On your table when you arrive, you'll find a bottle of local olive oil from Les Mées, the bottle we had boasting a top prize at the Concours Général de Paris of 1995. The butter comes wrapped as a cracker. There are three choices of menus. Perhaps the eight-course *menu découverte* (295F) might be a bit much for a touring lunch. The *menu du marché* is the simple three-course

option. This is reasonably good value as long as you like all three dishes proposed. The day we were there it was superb: *salade de moules en escabèche*, followed by *magret de canard aux figues*, finished off by a *feuilleté aux mirabelles*. The four-course *menu carte* (210F) offers a fairly manageable choice of four or five dishes per course.

Country bread is baked fresh every day here. Slightly decorated, it is light and tasty, and accompanied our *amuse-bouche*, very smooth fish *rillettes* in a gazpacho sauce, with a decoration of citronella leaves sticking out like green bunny rabbit ears. Several of the herbs Sylvain uses are grown in the back garden.

The starters came on Marseille plates with blue and yellow borders. The *aïoli froid de soles, pommes de terre à la crème de ciboulette* proved a neat reworking of the Provençal *aïoli* classic, presented here as a fresh vegetable *terrine* bound together by sole, the fish cooked to be quite firm. Peas, carrots and beans are caught within this fish wrapping. Creamy potatoes flavoured with chives and cream of carrots accompanied this. Otherwise you could have gone for a tomato *tartare* turning Spanish in its gazpacho, an old French favourite meeting Italy (not that far away now) in the *ravioles d'escargots de la Robine à la fondue de fenouil*, or a French classic with a touch of India in the *terrine de foie gras de canard réalisé par nos soins, chutney de poires*.

The main courses are paraded into the room hiding under silver lids. Marie announces the dishes and lifts the lids dramatically for an added touch of excitement. The aromas immediately fly out. The pigeon, though it won't have been fetched down from Le Vieux Colombier's own pigeon-loft, comes from nearby Ganagobie and is very highly recommended indeed. An article in a professional cookery magazine wrote once of Sylvain Nowak 'having a passion for pigeon which he finds very difficult to disguise'! Good pigeon tastes almost as rich and melting as good liver. It should be very little cooked and here a trickle of blood ran crimson from the bird as the fork went into it. Local Lurs mushrooms accompanied it. *Sarriette*, or savory, a herb found a good deal in the region, with tiny whitish, mauve-tinged flowers, decorated the plate. The duck came with figs, a delicious subtle sweet addition, delicately honeyed. The figs, from the garden, had been warmed in butter. Fish is a particular speciality of Sylvain Nowak's. With the *dos de morue en deux façons* dish you get two in one, cod panfried and salt cod as a *brandade*. The bass was panfried and served with *tomates confites* and a caviar of aubergines. Or you might be tempted by a *marinière* of *langoustines*, some *moules* and basil thrown in. For the more adventurous, among the meat dishes were calves' sweetbreads in a Port and capers sauce.

The oversized cheese trolley which Marie negotiates round the *bergerie* is the heavy goods vehicle model of its type. It holds a vast choice. 'Would you like a piece of each?', someone quipped. There are literally dozens. Ewe's and goat's appropriately enough, plus some cow's, although you don't see many of those creatures in the region. There are also those dangerously powerful types of goat's cheese dipped in *gniole*, or *marc*, and then wrapped in chestnut leaves.

You may be asked to order your pudding at the start of the meal to allow time for preparation. The choice is short but sweet. The *flan de marron* was a melting chestnut custard with an orange sauce, while the pear crumble was made out of the ordinary by the addition of praline and a kirsch *sabayon*. *L'aumonière aux pommes* seemed an appropriate dessert for the day, the apples in almond cream wrapped up in a pastry parcel in the shape of purses that pilgrims used to carry.

Fricassée de Lotte et Pistes aux Artichauts Barigoule

Serves 4–6

5 artichokes
500ml/¾ pint olive oil
125g/5oz carrots, peeled and thinly sliced
2 small onions, thinly sliced
1 tablespoon white wine
2 garlic bulbs, broken into cloves, cloves peeled
300g/11oz prepared baby squid
1 ½kg/4lbs monkfish fillets
salt and pepper

Fry the artichokes in a little of the oil. Fry the carrots and onions gently in some of the olive oil. Add the artichokes, deglazed with the white wine, plus the garlic cloves, and cover with all but a third of the remaining olive oil. Leave to cook for 20 minutes.

Wash the squid thoroughly inside and out under cold running water. Sauté the baby squid in a pan with the monkfish fillets. In a large serving dish, arrange the monkfish and the baby squid, the artichokes, cut into quarters, the carrots and the onions, then top with the reduced cooking juices from the artichokes, adjusting the seasoning with salt and pepper.

---

touring around

You might like to start your morning in **Manosque**, or to avoid it altogether if you don't like the look of it. It's ironic that Provence's greatest defender o]at the **Priory of Ganagobie**, a short distance north of Lurs, again high up on the Durance valley's heights (*inside of the priory only open after lunch, closed Mon*). The priory was founded in the 9th century as a dependency of Cluny. The remarkable church, which you reach via a picturesque *borie,* was built some 200 years later. Its portal, though reconstructed in the 1600s, still has its original *tympanum* relief: a *Christ in Majesty with the four Evangelists,* one of the finest such works in Provence. The 12 apostles stand under the flowing-haired Jesus in his mandorla, some single, some in pairs. Bent, fluted columns, little faces above the foliage on the outer capitals and the jigsaw pieces of the entrance make this an extraordinary façade. Inside is a further rare decoration, mosaics with geometric designs and peculiarly styled animals done in red, black and white.

The religious theme continues 5km north past Peyruis. Look out for signs to the church of **St-Donat**, in a wonderful setting on a little wooded plateau. This graceful building, dating from the 11th century, is one of the earliest Romanesque monuments in Provence. It was constructed for pilgrims visiting the relics of St Donat, a 5th-century holy man from Orléans who ended his life as a hermit here.

St-Auban down in the valley brings you not to another saint's church, but shockingly back into the postwar age with its petro-chemical factories and chimneys. Just beyond, **Château-Arnoux** has one stop for the major culinary pilgrim in Provence, La Bonne Etape. It has managed to keep the modern monstrosities to the south out of sight, set in its idyllic spot.

You can cross the Durance below St-Donat to come rapidly to **Les Mées** (Provençal for milestones). Les Mées is a pretty enough village, its narrow streets crushed into its narrow hillside setting. But the major attraction is the 2km of peculiar needle-like rock formations eroded into weird shapes north along the D4. They're known as the Pénitents des Mées, as though they were great cowled monks. The story goes that these monks were petrified (as in transformed into rocks) to punish them for lusting after female slaves whom a local lord was supposed to have brought back from the crusades.

The D4 joins the **Route Napoléon** north of Les Mées. This road name commemorates the devious way the terrifying megalomaniac took in 1815 on his return to France from exile on Elba in order to reach Paris and reclaim power, be it fleetingly. One hundred days after his triumphant arrival in Paris he lost the Battle of Waterloo. Follow his route briefly backwards along the stretch to Digne.

The Alps north of Digne are starting to look imposing. **Digne** itself (although the word means dignified in French) isn't quite so splendid. The capital of the Alpes-de-Haute-Provence, and the only city in a long stretch of mountains between Orange and Turin, over in Italy, Digne has one thriving boulevard of cafés and touristic knick-knackery mixed with smart shoe shops, posh chocolates and more than one bookshop, and has recently rediscovered its role as a spa.

Out of town (27 Avenue du Maréchal Juin) is something entirely unexpected: the **Fondation Alexandra David-Neel** (*guided tours with her former secretary, daily in summer at 10.30, 2, 3.30 and 5, otherwise at 10.30, 2 and 4*), the former home of a truly remarkable Frenchwoman who settled here in her 'Himalayas in miniature' after a lifetime exploring in Tibet. Ms David-Neel called this house Samten Dzong, the 'castle of meditation', and Tibetan Buddhist monks attended her when she died here. The Dalai Lama has since come twice to visit; there are exhibits of Tibetan art and culture, photographs, and also Tibetan crafts on sale.

At St Benoit, also a little out of the town centre, the **Geology Centre** (*open 9–12 and 2–5.30, 4.30 Fri; closed Sat and Sun April–Nov*) houses the largest geology collection in Europe. Leave the car below and walk up the hill by the big cascade. The displays may inspire you to visit the Réserve Naturelle Géologique de Haute Provence, the largest geological reserve in Europe, and to go searching for that fossilized ichthyosaurus.

The alternative route between Manosque and Digne to the busy one we've followed above takes you through the unspoilt **Asse valley**. You can make your own discoveries taking some of the dramatic side-roads up out of the valley. These tracks can be dangerous as you can see scrutinizing the Michelin map of Provence—many of them are signalled as 'of doubtful quality', so take care! Such tortuous little roads as the D17 from south of Mézel to Majastres (where wild roses run riot in June) take you to places lost in time, untouched by the modern world.

Gorging Yourself away from the Gorges du Verdon

Riez

Valensole, a mature old overgrown village on the edge of a great lavender-growing plateau, lies midway between Manosque and Moustiers-Ste-Marie. While Moustiers, one of the prettiest villages in France, shouts out its beauty from its spectacular cliff-side setting at the western end of the Grand Canyon du Verdon, Valensole seems to lack self-confidence. It hides secretively against its hillside. Climb to the top of it and you realize that the place is quite substantial and really quite beautiful. And unlike Moustiers, it isn't overrun with tourists. Mind you, it doesn't have quite the number of attractions of Moustiers, the latter with its most glamorous of locations, the most refined of ceramics, the most atmospheric of old churches, the prettiest of central cafés and the grandest canyon in Europe just nearby.

The flat, barren-looking plain of Valensole is an *haut lieu* of *lavande* and comes into its own when the lavender is in full colour in July. Almond trees, planted here in good number, bring an earlier rush of colour to the plain when they burst into flower in the spring. On your day out in the region, stick to the small Roman remains at Riez close to Valensole and then maybe go and look at the southern end of the absurdly artificially coloured waters of the Lac de Ste-Croix.

getting there

Valensole, between the Durance and the Grand Canyon du Verdon, hides along the D6, the latter a pretty poxy road connecting Manosque and Riez. Le Grand Hôtel is on the Place Frédéric Mistral down at the foot of the town, practically opposite the *mairie* or town hall.

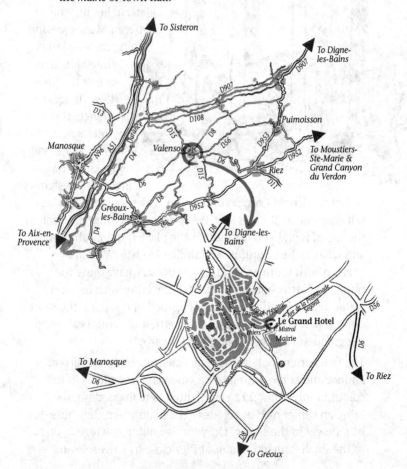

Le Grand Hôtel, Valensole

Le Grand Hôtel, 04210 Valensole, ✆ 04 92 74 89 24, 📠 04 92 74 89 24.
Closed Fri and Sun evenings and 25 Dec–31 Dec. Menus at 80F, 138F,
163F, 195F and 300F (truffle menu).

M. de Geeter was thrown into the cooking profession in his youth, and
very happy he seems about it too. From the age of 12 he learnt something of his craft with friends of his parents who held a restaurant.
Since those early days he has done his *tour de France*, his apprentice-
ship in various reputed establishments around the country. But his
cooking, you won't be surprised to learn given his early training, is
good old traditional French.

The exterior of Le Grand Hôtel may not be very grand, but the short
line of cafés and shops at the end of which it stands and the terrace
extending out to the town hall on the other side give the street on
which it lies some atmosphere. The de Geeters have managed this place
since 1987. They are unassuming and soft-spoken, clearly caring deeply
about the cooking and the service. The principal dining room has
peachy, brick and brown colours, paisley wallpaper and ochre curtains.

Pottery is going to turn out to be a bit of a theme for this suggested
lazy day, so if you like the plant holders with their coarsely executed
designs and intriguing mix of yellow, green and brown glazes, ask the
de Geeters how to find Gérard the village potter. The black and white
photos on the walls are inspiring—mysterious interpretations of the
annual *transhumance* ritual, the sheep running through the town on
the way to new pastures, a handful of goats in their midst, as is the traditional way. One of the de Geeters' daughters has trained to paint
designs on pottery, and some of her delicate work is displayed on the
buffet in the dining room.

Returning to her father's work, you can choose from one of five
menus. If you don't have a big budget, M. de Geeter does a workers'
lunch, the simple *menu ouvrier*, for a very reasonable 80F. After that,
it's four courses all the way for the four gastronomic menus, at 138F,
163F, 195F and 300F. The last two carry special titles, the *menu de la
Provence gourmande* (pretty self-evident), and the *menu du caveur*
(explanation of that last word to follow).

What's more, all but the basic menu start with *tartines provençales*. *Tapenade* (M. de Geeter gets the produce from 80 olive trees of his own) or conserved peppers you may be familiar with as Provençal starters, but maybe not *sausson*. This *pommade* consists of a mix of almond paste, olive oil, fennel and anchovies. With the top two menus, as well as *tartines provençales*, before dessert you're offered a *préparation au dessert*.

The number of choices on all these menus is sensibly limited. With the 138F one, you get traditional dishes. Your hors d'oeuvre might be melon with sweet, honeyish Beaumes-de-Venise or *tomme de chèvre fraîche, émulsion de tomate et de basilic*, goat's cheese as creamy as a fromage frais. For the main course, you might face a decision between Bresse chicken fricasséd with wild mushrooms, Alps *pieds et paquets*, or a *brouillade à la truffe blanche d'été*, a much glorified scrambled egg, cream added of course as well as the summer truffles which impart a crunchy texture.

The hors d'oeuvre step up a gear on the next menu: raw ham with a homemade *confiture* of green tomatoes, a tangy accompaniment, or crisp French beans with crayfish tails, again offering an interesting contrast of textures. With the Provençal menu, real truffles put in their first appearance, either with poached eggs or with the artichoke salad. By the *menu du caveur*, however, things truffly start to get out of hand: by way of hors d'oeuvre it was either the *brouillade* with black truffles or, winning the prize for outrageously rich starter, fresh *foie gras* with truffles.

You may have noticed that truffles appear to be a bit of an obsession with M. de Geeter. As we were eating our meal, he came to explain some of the latest truffle-tracking techniques used by one of his suppliers. This man planted the special oaks generously infected with the correct fungal illness. He waited five years to find out around which trees the truffles had taken—they leave a burnt ring around the tree, where the grass won't grow. Three or four years later such trees are ready to give truffles. But the man in question hunts his truffles not with pigs, not with dogs, but with the most sophisticated of modern techniques. Have you guessed it? Yes, he uses special flies. '*Il les cave à la mouche!*' M. de Geeter explained enthusiastically, as we took another mouthful of food. These flies have a very superior sense of smell apparently. '*Caver*', by the way, is the technical term for truffle-hunting, hence the '*menu du caveur*', the menu of the truffle hunter.

Continuing with the truffle menu, a main course of *poularde de Bresse* accompanied by a *sauce hollandaise truffée* would seem to come close to gastronomic obscenity. But looking at it from a different angle, 300F for such a rich menu stuffed with truffles is a bargain not worth turning your piggy nose up at, so it might be tempting to go the whole hog if your liver can cope.

Other less ostentatious choices included simple *salade d'artichauts violets aux truffes et à l'huile d'olive*. The artichokes are finely chopped so as to have a raw celeriac crunchiness to them and intriguingly decorative twirling ends. They have an almost aquatic look and are mixed with truffle oil and a drop of lemon.

Alain Ducasse, one of France's most famous chefs, came to Le Grand Hôtel, tasted and apparently enthused about M. de Geeter's favourite way of preparing snails, the *cassolette d'escargots petit gris de la Robine au lard paysan*, with plenty of garlic, tomatoes and herbs thrown in to accompany the tenderly cooked creatures. They aren't in the least chewy as they can sometimes be. Other tempting-sounding main courses included the pigeon with cream of artichokes, the sea bass with basil, or the leg of lamb braised in Gigondas.

There's a generous choice of puddings. Back with the sheep, you could try the *faisselle de brebis* with a raspberry *coulis*. If you're still looking for something slightly richer, the *crème brûlée* with lavender honey might do you. Or for something more refreshing try roasted strawberries with fresh mint. For an exotic Provençal ending you could opt for the *fruits du soleil confits* (melons, figs, but also clementines) with an apricot sauce and roasted almonds.

Ragoût d'Agneau aux Truffes

If you can't quite stretch to truffles, add some chopped mushrooms to the pan with the potatoes for a humbler but still delicious meal.

Serves 4

1kg/2lbs 4oz shoulder of lamb
6 tablespoons olive oil
3 carrots, peeled and chopped
1 onion, chopped
250ml/8fl oz dry white wine
1kg/2lbs 4oz potatoes, peeled and chopped
bouquet garni (thyme, bay leaf, orange peel, parsley)
salt and pepper
150g/5oz fresh Valensole or other truffles

Take the lamb off the bone and chop the meat into small cubes. Reserve the bones. Brown the meat in 2 tablespoons of the olive oil, then set aside.

Brown the carrots and onion, together with some of the bones, crushed, in 2 tablespoons of the olive oil. Pour in the wine and cook until it has evaporated. Add some water (the same again as the contents of the pan). Leave to cook gently for 30 minutes. Then strain the sauce through a fine sieve.

Brown the potatoes in a frying pan in the remaining olive oil, and cover them with the juices from the lamb. Leave to cook for 5 minutes, then add the bouquet garni, salt and pepper. Finally, add the truffles.

---

touring around

Why not head for **Riez** in the morning? Riez, east of Valensole, is an old centre for lavender-distilling. Ruined medieval houses have been restored, and artists and potters have moved in. It's pretty but bustling, a good place to dawdle in. Riez was an important Celtic religious site, though it isn't clear exactly which deity it honoured. Testimonies to later piety can be seen at the western edge of town, thought to have been the centre of Roman-era Riez: four standing columns of a Roman Temple of Apollo, and a 6th-century baptistry that is one of the few surviving monuments in France from the

Merovingian era; octagonal, like most early Christian baptistries (after the original, in the Lateran at Rome), it has eight recycled Roman columns and capitals; all the rest was heavily restored in the 1800s.

From Riez it's a shortish drive to see the southern end of the **Lac de Ste-Croix** at Ste-Croix-de-Verdon. The colour of this and other Verdon lakes beggars belief. It looks as though it's been coloured in an artificial turquoise by a child. In the distance, on the other side of the lake, lie the hulking masses of the southern mountains concealing the Grand Canyon du Verdon.

But back to **Valensole** for lunch. If you want to explore the village, don't try driving into the labyrinth of *ruelles*, the tiny narrow streets at the top of Valensole. We almost got our car stuck there. Best walk around the maze, with the odd medieval house, the odd fountain and wash houses, and many an old doorway. The upper village's slightly abandoned air recalls certain mournful, quiet Spanish towns and villages lost in the hills of Andalucia. But the predominant colours of the place as you look down from the top at the packed hillside are gentle beiges and pinks. You could ask the de Geeters for recommendations for shops to find some of the lavender specialities, which include not just lavender honey and *lavandin*, lavender essence, but also *pâté à la lavande*! Almonds are another speciality.

After lunch, head for the pottery cliff-side of Moustiers-Ste-Marie. Decide whether you want to hit the shops of Moustiers before touring round the Grand Canyon. Remember that the shops normally shut at 7pm. If you don't want to go round the potters, you could head straight for the canyon trail and return for an evening drink to Moustiers. If you decide to do the whole canyon loop it'll take several hours—although the distances aren't great, the road is winding, other traffic slow, but most of all the views are distractingly vertiginous.

The most surprising thing about the **Grand Canyon du Verdon** is that it wasn't 'discovered' until 1905. The locals always knew about it, of course; agriculturally useless and almost inaccessible, the 21km gorge had an evil reputation for centuries, as a haunt of devils and 'wild men'. Even after a famous speleologist named Martel brought it to the world's attention at the beginning of the century, many Frenchmen weren't impressed. In the '50s the government decided to flood the whole thing for another dam (the tunnels they dug are still visible in many places at the bottom); when the plan was finally abandoned, it was for reasons of cost, not natural preservation.

The name 'Grand Canyon' was a modern idea; when the French became aware of its existence, comparisons with that grand-daddy of all canyons in Arizona were inevitable. It does put on a grand show: sheer limestone cliffs as much as a half-km apart, snaking back and forth to follow the meandering course of the Verdon; in many places there are vast panoramas down the length of it. Most of the best views are from the so-called Corniche Sublime (D71) on the southern side.

Moustiers-Ste-Marie will be familiar to anyone who haunts the museums of the Midi, as Moustiers in the old days was Provence's famous centre for painted ceramics. You can compare today's potters' efforts with the originals at the Musée de la Faïence, a small collection on Place du Presbytère (*closed Tues*). In the middle of the village is the deep-set 12th-century parish church with a kink in it. It is deeply dark inside, just lit by candles. Only the twee religious music spoils the tone. The church even has its own fine pottery collection in one side-chapel. The choir has the sweetest of intimate side-aisles.

Moustiers's other distinction is the Cadeno de Moustié, a 225m chain suspended between the tops of two peaks overlooking the village. A knight of the local Blacas family, while a prisoner of the Saracens during the Crusades, made a vow to put it up if he ever saw home again; the star in the middle comes from his coat of arms. The original (silver-plated) was stolen in the Wars of Religion, and a replacement didn't appear until 1957. A climb up under the chain will take you to the dramatically perched Chapelle Notre-Dame-de-Beauvoir.

Return to the square to one side of the parish church and the Chante Cigale (Singing Cicada) café for your evening drink. You sit in the shadow of a huge, bulging plane tree. A stream rushes down the little gorge dividing the village in two. The views onto the houses and rooftops show France at its most picturesque. Moustiers is definitely a romantic location for a meal, but don't hope for Le Grand Hôtel's prices. Staying in the church square, you would do very well at Les Santons or, down at the foot of the village, La Bastide de Moustiers can cook you up a memorable dinner.

A Taste of the Provençal Alps

Auberge du Parc

This is a journey up the lesser-known Verdon, northeast of the Grand Canyon. Castellane is the town that marks the eastern end of the great chasm, the towering rock above it distinguished by a great ruddy Virgin. From Castellane, the road along the bizarre Lac de Castillon makes for an unusual, even distinctly spooky trip. A secretive military installation and alarming waterside road signs awaken suspicions along the southern edge of the lake. Still more strangely, on the western side of the lake, the silhouettes of gaudy outsized statues glint in the sunlight, high on the hillside. This is Mandarom, or Mandarom Shambhasalem, to give it its more long-winded and pretentious title, the centre of the cult of Aumism, which supposedly takes ingredients from all the world religions and then melts them up into something totally tacky looking.

But the weirdness doesn't stop there. On the northern end of the lake you may well see great triangular-winged, multi-coloured birds circling in the skies way above. It turns out that St-André-les-Alpes, our destination for a meal, is a major resort for those aeronautical loonies, hang-gliders.

The roads north and east of St-André lead into major mountains, that to the east heading up into the *département* of the Alpes Maritimes, that to the north continuing up the now extremely peaceful Verdon valley.

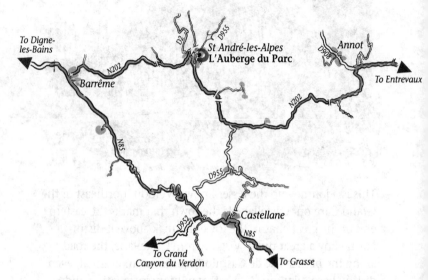

getting there

In the southeastern corner of the Alpes-de-Haute-Provence, a little way north of Castellane on the N202, St-André-les-Alpes has only one lively square and L'Auberge du Parc is well positioned on it, next to the church. On the other side of the church you'll find a big car park.

L'Auberge du Parc

L'Auberge du Parc, Place Charles Bron, 04170 St-André-les-Alpes, ✆ 04 92 89 00 03, ✆ 04 92 89 17 38. Closed 1 Jan–15 Feb. Menus at 85F, 140F and 190F.

In the midst of all this bizarreness, L'Auberge du Parc offers a traditional family restaurant and a halt much appreciated by hang-gliders.

In summer you can eat on the picturesque terrace on the church square. This is the busy hub of the village—there's hardly anything else to see, which is probably why. Inside, L'Auberge du Parc is the kind of traditional French restaurant where you eat with a doe's head banged into the wall above you, its eyes peering imperviously out at the restaurant beyond, its spirit long departed for pastures new. The *buffet* with the built-in clock is surrounded by two ferrets and a fox—fear not, they too are stuffed. In summer, there's also the shady garden to enjoy at the back of the inn from which the place takes its name.

People must come from great distances to eat here, going by the place's capacity, although St-André seems in the middle of isolated country outside the tourist season. We actually ate here on a September evening, when it was full of life. Certainly we don't believe that all the middle-aged clientele were staying here for the hang-gliding, but the naff dance music was at times coming dangerously close to inciting them to dance a conga. L'Auberge du Parc is a busy place in all senses, with masses of crockery and copper pans to add to the stuffed animal wall decoration.

The family that runs the restaurant, the Ferriers, offer a very jovial welcome and impart atmosphere to the place. Monsieur arrived here when he was one year old, and by 1996 had been here 54 years. His parents ran the *auberge* before him and now his very friendly son does a great deal of the cooking. The latter has worked in Monaco and is also very keen on car racing. Raymonde, the joke-cracking waitress who looked after us most of the time, has worked here well over a decade.

The food is hearty, generous country cooking, with fresh ingredients and a few surprise elements. The day we went, M. Ferrier had been out in the morning picking the mushrooms we would taste later. The restaurant serves starved hang-gliders' portions. Some of these hang-gliders stay up in the air for six hours or more apparently, which makes them work up a healthy appetite.

For 85F you get a filling three-course meal, starting with the self-service *buffet de crudités* offering the usual French starters, *carottes rapées*, melon balls, *museau* (pig's snout salad), aubergines, and North African dishes such as *couscous* and chick peas. This might be followed by shoulder of lamb with a garlic cream sauce, or pork chops in sage. And to finish off a piece of homemade tart. The 140F menu gives you the added choice either of cheese or of pudding; on the 190F menu you get both.

The house salad, the *salade de l'auberge*, makes for an excellent *mélange*, with one culinary surprise. On the enormous base of varied lettuce leaves lie vermilion slices of *mouton fumé*, smoked mutton. M. Ferrier is supplied from a producer in Barcelonette, the major town in the northeastern corner of the Alpes-de-Haute-Provence. Having sampled this very tasty meat, not oversalted, but tasting rather like a mix between carpaccio and bacon, we thought that surely some British producers ought to have a go at producing it if they haven't already. The generous platter also includes slices of liver pâté, gizzards, mushrooms, olives, pine kernels, tomatoes, etc. On the 140F menu the other starter might be something more banal but popular, like a saveloy in pastry, which in a bite makes you think you're a lot nearer Switzerland and Germany than you are—but at St-André we have reached major mountains and the word *saveloy* apparently originates in Italy, not that far away in fact. On the four-course menu, more refined French starters include stuffed mussels or snails.

mussels

We forgot to tell you about the boar's head on one of the restaurant's walls, but boar's meat did appear on the plate for main course, under the stewed guise of *civet de sanglier*. The accompanying spinach mousse was nicely flavoured with nutmeg. Good classic French dishes make up the bulk of the main courses on offer. On the 140F menu, you could go for a steak, choosing one of three traditional sauces to accompany it, or for the *gigot d'agneau à la crème d'ail*. The fillet of trout was made to sound more glamorous than normal with the addition of *sauce aux sanguins*, the latter the mushrooms M. Ferrier had picked a crate of that day. The *civet de sanglier* featured on the more expensive menu as did a *roulade de lièvre maison*.

Most of the puddings are fairly standard, *flan maison aux oeufs*, *île flottante*, fresh fruit and so on. You might be tempted by a *tarte aux myrtilles*. Blueberries are often to be found growing wild around mountain lakes. A sign painted on the front of the restaurant advertises it as a *Glacier*, but ices are no longer made as a matter of course on the premises. However, the *sorbet génipée* is interesting, flavoured with a little berry that only grows at high altitude, apparently—from 2000 metres up! M. Ferrier sometimes goes and picks them too. To end the meal, he offered us some liqueur made from these berries, described as '*la vieille liqueur des Alpes françaises*'. It looks like liquified lemon-curd, and it tasted both a bit almondy and a bit minty, a bizarre taste for a bizarre day.

La Fricassée de Porc St-Andréenne

Serve this hot, accompanied by jacket potatoes.

Serves 4

1kg/2lbs 4oz onions, thinly sliced
3 tablespoons olive oil
1kg/2lbs 4fl oz very lean pork, cut into 2cm/¾in cubes
1 sherry glass of marc de Provence
1 litre/1 ¾ pints good red wine
thyme
1 bay leaf
salt and pepper
200g/7oz liver, cubed
1 tablespoon flour
toasted slices of pain de campagne or bloomer

Fry the onions in 2 tablespoons of the olive oil until they are golden in colour. Add the meat and brown this too. Flambé with the marc. Add the red wine, herbs and salt and pepper. Leave to simmer gently for 1 hour.

Meanwhile, brown the liver in 1 tablespoon of the olive oil. Add to the meat and continue to cook for 10 minutes. Finally, add the blood left on the plate the liver was on, mixing the flour into it.

Arrange the toasted slices of bread on warm plates, and pour the pork fricassée over them.

touring around

You should have plenty to gossip about over lunch if you've spent the morning coming up from **Castellane**. Castellane is a village that has become the capital of the Grand Canyon, the base for visiting one of the greatest natural wonders in Europe. It's centred round a pretty square of plantains (the grilles surrounding the trees are worked in the shapes of plantain leaves) where *boules* is played, and people amiably hang about. But its edges are deep in up-to-the-minute sports shops supplying slick whizz-gimmickry for any sport you could or couldn't conceive of (such as bungee-jumping). If you penetrate into the other shops you'll find nothing you didn't expect: lavender, nougat, honey and *faïence*. Castellane has a pretty *mairie* and a church from behind which begins the 182m ascent of its famous rock: pick up the key for the chapel on top from outside the *curé*'s house, or collect it on your way up from the last person coming down.

Take the D995 north from Castellane for the Lac de Castillon and St-André-les-Alpes. As you reach the southern tip of the lake, turn onto the D402 for the western side to go and cast a glimpse at **Mandoram**. Once you've climbed up to this bizarre sect's amusement park of a religious site, a Barbie Doll Virgin carrying a ray-gun greets you at the entrance gates. Mandoram Shambhasalem apparently means Holy Mountain. You might not like to try Aumism yourself, but you can actually visit the village most afternoons. The aims of the sect, written on placards around the place, sound humanitarian and virtuous enough: to give people balance of body and mind; to let them understand themselves so that they can understand others; to pray for the evolution of human beings; to help mankind to progress... But the architecture of Mandoram smacks of the phoney, the self-aggrandizing, the deluded. Various monuments pay their respects to various holy places for different religions. Crowns litter the hillside, sticking into the air like so many kitchen whisks. The statues look like they're fake papier mâché or even *pâtisserie* figures. Among the giant effigies of the leaders of the world religions, you may not recognize one figure in particular. That'll be the Aumist leader, Sa Sainteté le Seigneur Hamsah Manarah, Premier Hiérokarantine, who has apparently revealed himself to be the Messie Cosmo-Planétaire awaited by so many. This may come as news to you. At the time we visited, he was defending himself in court against accusations of rape.

Go back down the hillside and along the eastern edge of the **Lac de Castillon**. Its great dam, the Barrage de Castillon, a mighty 89m concrete construction begun in 1942 under the Vichy government, has a distinctly grim wartime look about it. Past the military zone and placards, you can concentrate fully on the fascinating unreal colour of the lake, sheer hillsides dropping into it from the western side. At St-Julien-du-Verdon you come to a little lake-side resort.

You soon approach **St-André**. The area around is so highly regarded for hang-gliding that in 1991 the world championships were held here. There isn't that much to see in St-André itself. The main square outside L'Auberge du Parc is the main attraction. You can buy Génépi, that strange liqueur; or then an apéritif made with *myrtilles*. You might like to cast an eye over the church with its yellow front and neoclassical doorway. Plaques on the façade recall the Nazi execution of *maquisards*, Resistance fighters, in front of it.

In the afternoon, continue east to **Entrevaux**, the strategic key to the Var valley. There has been a fort of some kind here since Roman times, and its present incarnation is particularly impressive—the work of Louis XIV's celebrated engineer Vauban, standing guard high up on the cliffs above the village, complete with Second World War additions. At the time it was built the French-Piedmontese border was only a few miles away (it is now the departmental boundary between the Var and the Alpes-Maritimes). The entrance is a fortified bridge, rebuilt by Vauban on medieval foundations. Around the village, vestiges of its old garrison days can be seen: barracks and powderhouses, and an ancient drawbridge, still in working order, behind the 17th-century cathedral. The serious part of the fort is a hard fifteen-minute climb if you're fit; take iron rations, a sunhat and some historical imagination. A small fee should get you through the turnstile and after that hard climb you're on your own to explore the deliciously dangerous and derelict tunnels and dungeons. This little afternoon foray takes you to the edge of the Parc National du Mercantour and the border with Italy, but that's a whole different story.

Unspoilt Villages of the Northern Var

We come down into the *département* of the Var here, where we stay for the last three chapters of the book. The bulk of the Côte d'Azur lies in the Var, but we keep our haughty distance from all that glitzy glamour, even though it's never far away if you want to pop down to take a critical look at it, or to participate just a little. On the azure coast you can find the exciting buzz and bustle of the resorts, but in summer you'll also find huge traffic jams for commuting beachgoers and vast crowds. Separated from all that built-up brouhaha by the dramatically coloured Massif des Maures and the dividing line of the A8 'Provençale' motorway, the northern half of the Var has a quieter, wilder atmosphere.

Le Thoronet Abbey

Montfort-sur-Argens, the somnolent village our first Var day takes you to for lunch, is quieter than most. Northeast of it, you'll find a patch of pretty villages to explore—Cotignac and Tourtour stand out. Brignoles's bizarre museum and the sober Abbaye de Thoronet are the attractions in the major bauxite mining territory near Montfort.

getting there

Brignoles, on the N7, and with an exit from the A8 motorway, is the nearest town to Montfort-sur-Argens. This very peaceful village lies north of the motorway. The D554 runs north from Brignoles.

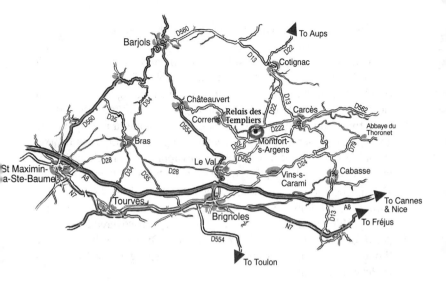

At Le Val just north of the motorway head east a few km along the D562 towards Carcès and then branch off onto the D22 for Montfort. The restaurant is on the corner of a discreet little square in the middle of the village.

Le Relais des Templiers

Le Relais des Templiers, Place G. Péri, 83570 Montfort-sur-Argens, © 04 94 59 55 06, ✆ 04 94 59 58 76. Closed Tues. Simple weekday lunchtime menu at 70F. Otherwise price depends on what Suzon has bought and ranges from 105F–185F.

Montfort-sur-Argens is a really, really sleepy village, in fact a village that has seemingly been drained of most of its life. But quiet can be a blessing for those of you who've been caught in the frenzy of the Côte d'Azur. Suzanne Hézard, or Suzon as she's more commonly known, who runs the Relais des Templiers pretty well single-handedly, seems to be the heart and soul of Montfort to anyone visiting briefly. She says she finds it too quiet here, lively as she is. She has lived in the village since the mid-1970s, actually dragged down south with her husband by an unfortunate business scam. But they stayed and she decided to open the restaurant in the early 1980s.

Her restaurant is tiny. The dining room on the street corner only has five tables. On summer evenings, Suzon puts out some tables and chairs in the little square outside, but in the midday heat she doesn't do so, feeling that it would be uncomfortable. (There are actually a couple of vaulted rooms down below, reserved for big occasions.) You clearly need to phone to reserve a table given the limited space. At the same time, you should ask what may be on the menu the day you're going, and let her know if there's anything you particularly dislike. Suzon's is a very friendly, warm, generous approach to receiving guests, but, as in a family home, the choice of food will be very restricted.

The dining room has a homely feel. A school desk stands in one corner, with a Robert Carrier book on it. And there in its pages is a large profile of Suzon. So this isn't quite an undiscovered backwater. Suzon describes Carrier as her *ange gardien*! Or perhaps he might be thought of as a knight in shining armour, a blessing for the fortunes of Le Relais des Templiers.

Why the reference to the medieval Knights Templars? The village may have been a location for the knights' secret training. There's a map of the 'Var Templier' on the wall, giving the locations of the old *commanderies*, farms and landholdings of the massively powerful bankers for the crusades, wiped out at the start of the 14th century. A painting of a knight and brashly coloured crusading scenes can be spotted around the restaurant walls. The *Var Village Voice* newsletter gives an indication that even if the Knights Templars were eradicated in medieval times, the English have a firm foothold today.

 To the cooking. The starter for us was a *terrine de foie de volaille*, a well-balanced, satisfying pâté. We also helped ourselves to some of the mushrooms *à la grecque* Suzon had prepared. At other times she might make *rillettes* with ducks or rabbits, or a *soupe au pistou*, some of her favourite starters.

It being the hunting season when we were visiting Suzon, she served us boar for the main course. Rather than a stew with lumps of *sanglier* meat as you often get, here she served the wild beast in thin slices, with a creamy celeriac purée. To add some sweetness to the strong flavour of the game, she put a touch of chutney in the madeira sauce, which also contained raisins and pine nuts. Suzon also likes to cook venison, say in an Armagnac sauce, accompanied by redcurrant jelly—

the jams here are homemade. Or you might taste one of the tradi-tional Provençal dishes such as a *daube* or an *aïoli*. *Pieds et paquets* may be for a bolder clientele.

Suzon is very happy to accommodate vegetarians. '*Je trouve que ça me simplifie la vie,*' she says good-naturedly. (It's necessary to give her advance warning, of course.) She might then do such dishes as *crêpes aux champignons*, *ratatouille* with poached eggs on top, or big salads with hot goat's cheese and pine nuts.

Sometimes regulars put in requests. For example, her *soufflé au fro-mage* is a bit of a favourite. But Suzon explains that '*J'aime bien improviser*', when asked about how she decides what to cook. She doesn't have a deepfreeze or a microwave oven in her kitchen, she proudly explains. Local markets she can go to include the Saturday ones at Brignoles and Carcès and the Tuesday ones at Cotignac and Lorgues. The last she describes as '*immense et superbe*'.

The puddings are traditional. Mainstays on her menus include *char-lottes*, crème caramel, rice pudding, chocolate mousse, filled *crêpes*, or *gâteaux* using Provençal fruits, such as a *pêchier*. There were also meringues cooking in the oven on the afternoon we were there.

We drank a Domaine de Fontainebleau, a fruity white, not from a Parisian château, but from a property in the sea of vines on the out-skirts of Montfort. It turns out that Suzon's son works there.

La Tarte aux Pignons du Bastidon

Serves 4

125g/4½oz flour
75g/3oz fat (half butter and half lard)
2 tablespoons blackcurrant jelly
450ml warm crème pâtissière
2 tablespoons ground almonds
100g/4oz pine nuts

Prepare a shortcrust pastry by blending the flour and fat together, then adding tablespoonfuls of cold water and mixing until the mixture forms a smooth dough. Leave to rest in a cool place for 30 minutes or longer. Preheat the oven to 200°C/400°F (gas mark 6).

Roll out the pastry. Grease a tart or cake tin 20cm/8in in diameter and line it with the pastry. Coat the bottom of the pastry case with the blackcurrant jelly, then with the still just warm crème pâtissière. Dust with the finely ground almonds, sprinkle the pine nuts over the top, cover with foil, and bake in the preheated oven for about 30 minutes, removing the foil 10 minutes into the cooking time. To avoid the bottom of the pastry becoming too soft, you could first cook it on its own for 10 minutes and dust it very lightly with flour before adding the crème pâtissière.

touring around

First, some pretty villages to signal northeast of Montfort. You may be coming from the south, but here we take the route coming down from the Lac de Ste-Croix and the Grand Canyon du Verdon, skirting round the western side of the barren and distinctly creepy Canjuers, turned into a vast military training ground.

We very highly recommend a little detour to **Tourtour** just southeast of Aups. The advantage of arriving at Tourtour early on a totally clear morning is that from its heights you may have the thrill of spotting the sea, minute in the distance. Olive trees grow along with the plane trees on the main street. The ancient communal olive oil mill comes back into action each year in January, but in summer it's turned into an exhibition hall. It dates back to medieval times, Romanesque-looking in some aspects, probably altered in the 17th century. The ancient terraced fields whose traces you can see around the village are known as *restanques*. Water used to be carefully canalized around them centuries ago. Walk round the village and the two castles and up to the church. Tourtour is something of a culinary village. On your tour you might be tempted to shop at the wonderful gourmet delicatessen, Les Girandoles, which turns restaurant in the evening. Just outside the centre, the Bastide de Tourtour has a highly reputed restaurant blending Provençal and nouvelle cuisine.

Salernes looks splendidly ordinary after the beauty of Tourtour. It has been known for over 200 years as a manufacturer of tiles: the small, hexagonal terracotta floor-tiles called *tomettes* that are almost as much a trademark of Provence as lavender. They still make them, and in a day when French factory-made tiles generally come in insipid beige, they are at a premium. Lately Salernes's factories and individual artisans have been expanding into coloured ceramics and pottery; there are a few shops in the village and factory showrooms on the outskirts. With such a workmanlike background, the village itself is rather drab, with a medieval fountain and a simple 13th-century church.

Just west, **Sillans** has lately been calling itself Sillans-la-Cascade, to draw attention to the 36m waterfall just south of the village (it dries up in summer); beyond that **Fox-Amphoux** is worth a visit just to hear the locals pronounce the name; this minuscule and well-restored village of stepped medieval alleys sits on a defensible height. It has a ruined castle, and on the trail to the hamlet of Amphoux, an odd cave-chapel, Notre-Dame-de-Secours, hung with ex votos, many from sailors. The D13 and D560 westwards take you into deliciously drowsy landscapes, but rather than falling deeply into that dream world you should head on for lunch via Cotignac.

Its inhabitants might be unaware of it, but **Cotignac** is one of the cutest of the cute, a Sunday-supplement Provençal village where everything is just right. It has no sights, but one looming peculiarity: the tufa cliffs that hang dramatically over it. In former times these were hollowed out for wine cellars, stables or even homes; today there are trails up to them for anyone who wants to explore.

After lunch, make for the bizarre attraction of **Brignoles**. From Montfort, you could stretch out the journey into town by first meandering down the Argens valley to Correns and Châteauvert. This way you pass through the valley inundated by vines. Then you enter the gorge to Correns, a charming small-scale village, with little cliffs outside it which draw rock climbers.

On to Brignoles's rich regional museum. Situated at the top of the attractive old town, on Place du Palais des Comtes de Provence, in a palace that was those counts' summer residence, Brignoles's incredible curiosity shop, the Musée du Pays Brignolais (*closed Mon and Tues, otherwise 9–12 and 2.30–6; adm*), has grown to fill the whole building since a local doctor began the collection in 1947. Amidst two big floors packed full of oil presses, fossils, cannon-balls, reliquaries and roof tiles, you'll see some things you never dreamed existed. In the place of honour, near the entrance, is the original model of a great invention by Brignoles's own Joseph Lambot (1814–87): the steel-reinforced concrete canoe. Admittedly a hard act to follow, but just across the room is a provocative sarcophagus, dated c. AD 175–225, nothing less than the earliest Christian monument in France. It is believed to be Greek, possibly made in Antioch or Smyrna; how it got here no one knows.

Try to avoid the big N7 road east to the **Abbaye de Thoronet**. The abbey (*open Mon–Sat 9–7 summer, 9–12 and 2–5 Sun, 10–12 and 2–5 winter; adm*) was the first Cistercian foundation in Provence, built on land donated by Count Raymond Berenger of Toulouse in 1136; the present buildings were begun about 1160. Like most Cistercian houses, it was in utter decay by the 1400s; and like so many other medieval monuments in the Midi, it owes its restoration to Prosper Mérimée, Romantic novelist (author of *Carmen*, among others) and State Inspector of Historic Monuments under Napoleon III.

It often seems as if the restoration is still under way; you may find parts of the abbey full of props, scaffolding and concrete piers, as its keepers experiment desperately to keep Thoronet from being shaken to pieces by the bauxite lorries rumbling past on the D79. The mines themselves (nearby, but screened by trees) have caused some subsidence, and cracks are opening in the walls. The place displays sophisticated Romanesque architecture stripped to its bare essentials, with no worldly splendour to distract a monkish mind, only grace of form and proportion. The elegant stone bell tower would have been forbidden in any other Cistercian house (to keep local barons from commandeering them for defence towers), but those in Provence got a special dispensation—thanks to the *mistral*, which would have blown a wooden one down with ease. There are no such compromises in the blank façade, but behind it is a marvellously elegant interior; note the slight point of the arches, a hint of the dawning Gothic—Thoronet was begun in the same year as France's first Gothic churches, in the north at St-Denis and Sens.

A Military Meal away from the Glamour of St-Tropez

Fashion victims might say that Les Arcs-sur-Argens lies on the wrong, northerly side of the Massif des Maures, the famous ochre-filled hills that run behind St-Tropez. Here we try to encourage you to keep north of the Massif des Maures. You'll be able to tour major French military territory this way. The town of Draguignan is the biggest military base in France. In the great bleak hills a little further north, the Camp Militaire de Canjuers stretches over a vast expanse. But it's worth heading up into this unfriendly territory to reach the perched little village of Bargème above it. Other pretty villages such as Lorgues, Flayosc, Comps-sur-Artuby, Bargemon and Callas lie along our trail.

The restaurant Le Logis du Guetteur has turned a former military post into a wonderful *cadre*. It has taken over the medieval fort at the top of Les Arcs. You see so many hilltop castle ruins in Provence that it's good to be able to find one in which you can eat.

Le Logis du Guetteur

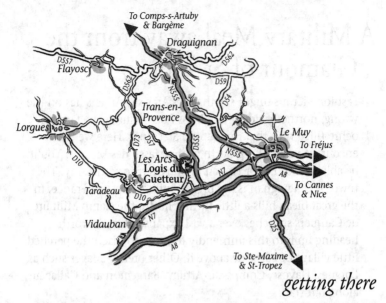

getting there

The hotel is very visibly perched on the little town's hillside, which isn't far from the A8 motorway exit for Draguignan. If you're coming off the motorway, then join the N7 heading west and turn north off it for Les Arcs-sur-Argens. If you're coming south from Draguignan, watch out carefully for the Les Arcs turning off the busy N555. Le Logis du Guetteur lives up to its name, which means 'the lookout's lodge'. You can see the slim square keep from far away, so you simply have to head for that. Parking space is very tight up in the old village. If you're lucky you may find a spot on the cobbled car park right by the keep, on the very roof supporting the vaulted dining rooms!

Le Logis du Guetteur

Le Logis du Guetteur, Place du Château, 83460 Les Arcs-sur-Argens, © 04 94 73 30 82, ® 04 94 73 39 05. Closed 20 Jan–1 March. Menus at 135F, 199F and 280F.

The transformation of a military castle into a fine hotel-cum-restaurant is surely one of the greatest signs of progress in civilization. Le Logis du Guetteur is therefore doubly wonderful, for its symbolism as well as its aesthetics. You might prefer to come and eat here at night to appreciate its magnificent setting to the full. Vaulted chambers have been converted into intimate dining rooms. Otherwise you can eat on the terraces perched on one side of the castle. They lie close to the little swimming pool (not an original feature) and look out over the roofs of Les Arcs and a bell tower capped by a construction that looks like a German helmet. From the poolside you can hear the noises coming from the kitchen. But the vaulted chambers are the best place to eat.

At the back of the voluminous menu you can read the briefest of histories of the castle. It dates as far back as the 12th century. The slim keep after which the place is now named, made of pinkish sandstone blocks, is from the 13th century. The place was devastated in warring. In more recent times, its dark chambers served for mushroom farming. One of the vaulted rooms has been converted into a bar. Here the owner, Max Callegari, showed us a secretive opening penetrating the thick walls to the well, and a groove to evacuate water. He thinks that his bar was once the castle's wash room.

Max's father converted the place in 1970, taking it on a lease for 99 years at 100F a year. Max is now the calm and friendly presiding figure. His wonderful surname, which sounds like a character in one of Shakespeare's Italian-inspired plays, indicates certain family roots. Max trained at an *école hôtelière* in Nice. He also spent a year working at the Shakespeare hotel and for the Royal Shakespeare Company—he was once married to an Englishwoman.

The three-course menu at 135F is relatively simple. For 199F you get a wide choice for each of the three courses. Add another 25F for the *assiette de fromages fermiers* and you could have a four-course meal. The 280F menu contains additional frills.

The wine list is extensive. Divided by region, each viticultural area of France is presented with a gushing line or rhyme, a troubadour touch singing the praises of each. We opted for a Bouches-du-Rhône, Les Genêts 1995. It turned out that it's produced by the Marquis de Villeneuve-Flayosc, who is descended from Raimond de Villeneuve, the lord who was originally granted feudal permission to build Le Logis du Guetteur's castle. The wine is pale-coloured, with a bouquet of flower blossoms and a refreshing taste. You may have spotted some vines on the stony ground above Les Arcs and might like to try the local Château Ste-Roseline. Not only does that estate produce good wine; it is also graced with a chapel with a Chagall mosaic, making it doubly worth visiting.

The side-plates are stamped with a crest, of course. The main courses come on silver platters. There are amusing touches to the decoration of the walls of what one imagines were once pretty grim chambers. The crossed weapons and the pictures of knights go with the surrounds. As do some of the little spot lights that you could envisage being turned to good use for torture interrogation. Our comfortable rounded green chairs contrasted with the pink table cloths.

The cuisine in this military setting is gentle and sophisticated. The 135F menu would certainly satisfy most. You might spot the odd Italian touch, for example in the salmon with avocado, served in cannelloni. The salad of smoked duck *magret* came with rather curious melon gelatine and neatly torn leaves. It being autumn and the mushroom season, there were ceps ravioli on the menu. Moving to the main course, the quail almost had the richness of a pâté. The *jus de morilles* over it was a sauce packed with further delicious mushrooms. This heady mix was offset by simple cabbage, bacon and carrots. The salmon came with a fine mousse of fennel and leeks. Or you could go for the roast lamb accompanied by a *gratin* of aubergines.

The 199F menu is perhaps the one to focus on. For a light, crispy starter you could try the *beignets de fleurs de courgettes à la ricotta et aux herbes*. Salmon again appeared, marinated with soft spices. Other seafood dishes included a salad of haddock with chicory and potatoes, or crayfish in their bisque—luxurious choices for this price of menu. You could even try *foie gras mariné au Frontignan et sa compotée d'oignons aux poivrons*.

We tried the *rascasse en bouillabaisse*. This was not the full, complicated, authentic *bouillabaisse*. With the genuine article, when the fish are separated from the soup, having imparted the latter with all their tasty juices, they are often quite dry. But the scorpion fish here wasn't in the least worn. The sauce, with a good number of mussels thrown in in particular, wasn't overpowering, but the *rouille* on *croûtons* added a spicy note. The other fish dish was anglerfish with leeks. Some of the accompanying vegetables on this menu were particularly tempting. To go with the duck fillet in honey sauce, you could try a *tian*, where the vegetable used is baked with rice and egg.

The puddings were delicate, several extremely refreshing, such as the *terrine de fruits frais et son coulis d'orange*, the *pêches au coulis de vin et sorbet de fromage blanc*, or the *tarte fine de pommes*, over which you could melt the accompanying cinammon ice cream. This might be a good restaurant to try *tiramisu*. Or for chocolate enthusiasts, go for the *dôme au chocolat blanc et noisettes torréfiées*. As is often the case in French restaurants, the puddings are referred to here as *douceurs*, a word summarizing well the gentle charms of Le Logis du Guetteur.

Les Beignets de Fleurs de Courgettes à la Ricotta

Serve these stuffed courgette flowers with an aubergine and onion purée and a few leaves of rocket or salad leaves of your choice.

Serves 6

1 tablespoon chopped fresh dill
1 tablespoon chopped fresh chives
1 tablespoon chopped fresh parsley
200g/7oz ricotta
18 courgette flowers
4 eggs
150g/5oz flour
150ml/¼ pint milk
150ml/¼ pint beer
2 litres/ 3½ pints oil, for deep-frying

Mix the herbs in with the ricotta and then use to stuff the courgette flowers. Make a fritter batter by mixing the eggs with the flour, and then whisking in the milk and beer. Heat the oil, dip the stuffed courgette flowers in the batter then fry them in batches for 3 minutes. Drain well before serving.

touring around

OK, Les Arcs is only 30 kilometres away from **St-Tropez**, so if you *have* to go you could make a quick dash from there to see the place. A quick dash? In summer you can get caught in enormous coastal traffic jams which would make you liable to miss lunch. At least go very early in the morning, if you do go. St-Tropez and its *golfe* are still enchantingly beautiful. Once you've wandered a little along St-Tropez's coastal path and through the narrow lanes of chic boutiques, you could treat yourself to the luxury of an enjoyably expensive drink at one of the delightful cafés looking onto the *boules* players' plane-shaded square. Beautiful villages restored by wealthy fifth-, sixth- or seventh-home owners lie in the hills above St-Tropez, while chichi resorts like Port-Grimaud and Ste-Maxime crowd round the *golfe*.

For an alternative, wholly contrasting morning, lack of glamour guaranteed, head for **Draguignan** just a short distance north of Les Arcs. Draguignan gets a bad press: ugly, depraved, full of soldiers; avoid it if you can... It isn't French so much as French colonial. The army practically owns the place and its dusty palm-shaded boulevards pass the national schools of artillery and military science. The Saturday market is especially good, and there are a few things to see in town: the 17th-century Tour de l'Horloge, Draguignan's architectural pride; a small Municipal Museum with a picture gallery and *faïences* from Moustiers (as well as porcelain from China); and the Musée des Arts et Traditions Populaires. This offers a complete, didactic overview of everything you'll never see in the real Provence any more—from mules to silk culture, along with reconstructions of country life, including barns, kitchens, festivals and, naturally, some antique *boules* and *tambourins*.

In the afternoon, we'd propose a devious route heading north again, but avoiding Draguignan. To see that town twice in one day would be excessive. Instead, go westwards along the D10 to **Lorgues**. Clément Bruno of Chez Bruno is one of the characters of the Var, who has converted his family home in the neighbourhood into a much-loved restaurant, truffles a speciality. With a complete ensemble of 18th-century municipal decorations, Lorgues offers proof that the Ancien Régime wasn't quite so useless after all, with a fountain, the dignified church of St-Martin, and the inevitable avenue of venerable plane trees, one of the longest and fairest in Provence.

Weave your way back east to **Flayosc**, which preserves a defensive feel to it, its town houses like town walls. The place is slightly tatty, rather bare from the outside and within. Fountains give some life to it though, while for some solid country cooking you could try L'Oustaou. Pass through Rebouillon, beautiful in its valley, with a little theatre of terraces. You then come into the Gorges de Châteaudouble, apricoty patches on the rocks, big pines adding picturesque touches.

Past Montferrat and you enter the distinctly unwelcoming military grounds. Guns are none too subtly concealed at the **Camp de Canjur** base already high up in the hills. Don't leave your car in the chillingly barren country that follows. The signs are unnervingly forthright, with repetitive messages like '*Danger, Danger, Danger*', '*Danger de mort*' and '*Tir permanent*' (permanent shooting!).

Coming out above this nightmare, you reach Comps-sur-Artuby with two hilltop churches. Head east for **Bargème**, the highest perched village in the Var. It must once have been more important than it is now, to go by the stocky towers of the château that remain, the solid Romanesque church and the abandoned terracing to the west. These days most of the houses, reached via the two medieval gateways, only come to life in summer. A tiny vaulted chapel has been restored to the west of the village. Dominated by a seemingly flat-topped mountain, Bargème looks down from its height onto rows of wooded hills receding to the south.

A wiggling road leads you back south to **Bargemon**. It's profoundly dark like the military camp, but mainly because of the deep shade provided for its curving hillside streets and squares by its towering plane trees. A few wiggles more and you reach **Callas**, standing below a ruined castle. The D25 south from Callas as far as Le Muy provides a beautiful route through forests, with the Gorges de Pennafort and a waterfall along the way. This also turns into one of the best wine roads in the region. You could stop at one of the properties to sample their Côtes-de-Provence.

Looking Down on the Côte d'Azur from the Pays de Fayence

On the most crystal clear of mornings it's possible to see Corsica from the *village perché* of Mons in the northeastern Var. More likely you'll be able to make out tantalizing stretches of the Côte d'Azur from up there. Fréjus and St-Raphaël lie distantly to the south, Cannes to the southeast.

Head just a little south from Mons and you come into the pays de Fayence, pretty country, but one where you start to see the effects of the Riviera's rampant success, with lines of postwar villas poking out of the hillsides. Somehow you feel you're leaving the Provence of old villages which, even if many of their houses have been rejuvenated, have remained roughly untouched through time. Seillans, just west of bustling Fayence, has kept its splendid old heart going, though. We stop to eat at the popular Hôtel des Deux Rocs.

In the afternoon we suggest a trip to Grasse and around. The town is the perfume capital of the world. It's no surprise that Fragonard was a native, the most rosy of Ancien Régime

Hôtel des Deux Rocs

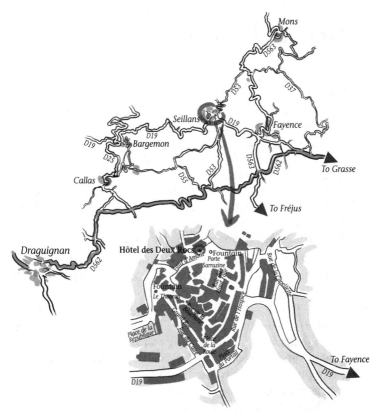

painters, with a particular predilection for portraying rosy-cheeked aristocrats on swings or skipping around rose gardens.

getting there

Little Seillans snails up its hill a handful of km west of Fayence along the D19. It's easiest to park to the west of the village, as otherwise you can get all too easily caught up in the narrow streets. Once parked, either walk along the curving higher street, the Route de la Parfumerie, to reach the Font d'Amont, or go down via the fountain square of Le Thouron and wend your way through the steep *ruelles* to emerge at the Porte Sarrazine, by the two rocks after which the hotel is named.

Hôtel des Deux Rocs

Hôtel des Deux Rocs, Place Font d'Amont, 83440 Seillans, © 04 94 76 87 32, ⚲ 04 94 76 88 68. Closed Tues lunch, Thurs lunch and Nov–March. Menus at 90F, 145F and 210F.

The Hôtel des Deux Rocs couldn't be described as shy and retiring. Not that it's loud; but it is quite well known. As far as a hotel can, it exudes an air of easy self-confidence. It has of course been a success—while a good number of the restaurants featured in this guide only started up in the early 1990s, the Deux Rocs has been going for over a couple of decades now. The day before we last went, Jean-Claude Van Damme, that Belgian piece of filmstar brawn, had been at the hotel during shooting for his latest film.

The Hôtel des Deux Rocs is successful because it has so many of the ingredients visitors expect of Provence. Its typical Provençal prettiness touches on the glamorous. With such a lovely atmosphere, such refreshing shade and such well-prepared food, it is a joy to stop here.

The Hôtel des Deux Rocs is run by a trio of characterful women. Francine, the manager, has something of a Money Penny air to her. She is sharp and sharp-witted, and, although you could imagine her being tart with fools, she is utterly charming in her welcome. The owner is Mme. Hirsch, a Parisian with whom Francine has worked since the hotel was opened in the early 1970s. We were looked after over lunch by Françoise, who once ran another restaurant in Seillans, and whose quiet attention was occasionally broken by an endearing smile and a charming comment.

The young chef, Thierry Brouard, arrived here in April 1996. Just previously he had been working down the road, and prior to that in Paris. He inherited the fine reputation established by the previous chef. Our food was all that you could wish for: light, elegant without being fussy, leaving us with a glow of wellbeing.

We were seated at one of the ten or so tables outside, by the fountain, from which the waiters draw water for your table. This fountain is topped by an obelisk on four balls, itself crowned by what looks like a stylized artichoke or pineapple. The plastic chairs can be slightly awkward to balance on the cobbles, so beware the grooves and make sure you're firmly ensconced before getting into lively conversation. Around the square you can see rocks, ivy-clad walls, an old *lavoir* in one corner, a wrought-ironwork stair balustrade to the house tucked in next to the hotel... The hotel façade is a gentle beige with blue-jeans-coloured shutters. Canvas chairs are placed on the thin terrace in front of the façade in summer, as well as white benches and olean-ders in terracotta pots. And then there are the two splendidly spreading plane trees, their dappled bark an abstract picture of greys, beiges and whites.

The *salade des Deux Rocs* makes an excellent starter. The *gambas,* which you have to pick up and peel, are deliciously grilled in walnut oil, the duck *magret* slices pleasantly salted, that taste playing off the lettuce leaves which are simply covered with oil, not vinegar. Smoked salmon pieces add to the colours, textures and tastes. On to another hors d'oeuvre, gizzards may present a problem to squeamish Anglo-Saxons, but they have a very smooth yet solid texture and a taste that isn't overpowering. You could try them in another salad option, liber-ally scattered with pine kernels. The leek tart is one of the best you're likely to taste, creamy, rich in taste, just nicely cheesy, but with all that still light. Other choices might include soups, but the best known hors d'oeuvre of the hotel is the *terrine aux légumes*, whose recipe is given below. Apart from the *salade des Deux Rocs*, these starters feature on the four-course 145F menu. The special salad is on the 210F menu. The other hors d'oeuvre on this more expensive menu are rather exclusive, including such delights as *coquilles St-Jacques* with garlic and almonds, and *foie gras* with pears.

We were drinking soft, slightly peachy Estaudon Blanc de Blanc, a wine from near Toulon, to accompany our meal. A feeling of bliss had rapidly descended upon us. We looked out over the hillside to be sur-prised by a couple of white teradactyles floating high in the sky, mimicking each other's languid movements. Our young assistant waiter informed us that they were gliders on white wings. Fayence is apparently the biggest gliding centre in Europe.

On to the main courses. Five white nuggets of monkfish were cooked to perfection, served in a *nage*, a beige transparent fish stock sauce.

Three pieces of garlic *en chemise* accompanied them. The tiny onions were so sweet that they came as close as an onion will to tasting like a grape. The chef is generous with the choice of *petite* vegetable accompaniments, such as spinach, broccoli in a little quiche or celeriac mousse. The monkfish was the most tempting *plat de résistance* on the more expensive menu. Again among the other choices, veal sweetbreads might have sounded a bit risqué for some, here served with a mustard grain sauce. The beef fillet came with a pepper one. Back with the 145F menu, the duck with honey was accompanied by a rich orange-coloured carrot sauce, the duck tender and melting. A *compote* of shallots cooked in Var wine added a touch of sweetness to the beef *onglet*, while the sea bass came in a velvet swimming crab sauce.

It became necessary to order a further bottle of wine. This time we opted for the Château Minuty Cuvée de l'Oratoire, which definitely has hints of apples. It comes from the St-Tropez peninsula, near Gassin, bottled in a comical model-curved bottle. A luggage label of a leaflet hanging from its shapely form invites you to go and visit the property.

The cheese dish was a yoghurty mousse of goat's cheese, with bits of basil and garlic chunks. Perhaps this dish could be considered French goat's cheese's answer to the American chocolate chip cookie? By way of a simple refreshing pudding, the fruit cocktail offered a chilled mix of melon balls, grapefruit pieces, pineapples, kiwis and peaches in an orange sauce. The *ganache au chocolat* tart, by contrast, was as rich as a caramel slice. The chocolate and vanilla sauce had pistachios in it. It is one of those puddings which are so good that they can make you lose all shame—some in our party were seen licking their plates. After coffee, a bell rang in the village, calling us to visit it.

Terrine aux Légumes

Make this terrine at least one day before you wish to serve it.

Serves 6–8

4 leeks

1kg/2lbs 4oz carrots

10 medium turnips

250g/9oz green beans

For the jelly:
25g/1oz butter
3 large onions
3 litres/5½ pints water
2 calf's feet
bouquet garni of a few sprigs thyme, 1 bay leaf, and a few sprigs parsley
1 egg
20g/¾oz gelatine, soaked in cold water
salt and pepper

For the mayonnaise:
500ml/17fl oz oil
2 egg yolks, at room temperature
1 tablespoon mustard
1–2 teaspoons white wine vinegar or lemon juice
a couple of sprigs parsley, chopped
4–6 chives, chopped
a few sprigs chervil, chopped

olive oil

Peel all the vegetables and wash them. Set aside the green parts of 2 of the leeks. Chop all but 2 of the carrots and all the turnips into thin batons about 5mm/¼in thick. Chop the leeks into 6cm/2½in lengths. Leave the green beans whole.

Cook all these vegetables separately in salted boiling water (for the carrots, add a little sugar to the water). Drain and rinse them under cold water. Set aside 2 tablespoons of carrots and 1 of the turnips to use in the sauce.

For the jelly, the following ingredients should be left to soften in the butter in a stewpot: the 2 reserved carrots, finely sliced, the set-aside green parts of the leeks and the onions, finely chopped. Add the water and the calf's feet and bring to the boil. Skim the surface, then drop in the bouquet garni. Simmer, covered, for 1½ hours.

Now strain the stock. Pick out the vegetables from the sieve and mash them or use a blender or food processor to do this so that you have a smooth purée. Set aside in the fridge. Next, return the strained stock to the pan and cook over a medium heat to reduce it by half. Skim the fat off. Add the egg, crushed and with its shell, to the stock and it should become clear. Boil again gently for 5 minutes, then strain once more. If the stock has not clarified enough, repeat this procedure.

Next add the gelatine, that you have been previously soaking in cold water and squeezing dry with your hands first. Stir and add salt and pepper to taste. Leave to cool and, as soon as it starts to thicken, pour a first layer of the jelly into the bottom of the mould or tin. Leave to set in the fridge.

Then arrange a layer of the cooked carrots, leeks and turnips, finishing with the green beans. Pour the rest of the jelly between the walls of the terrine or tin and the vegetables and over the top of them. Keep any jelly you have left over. Place the terrine and spare jelly in the fridge.

To make the mayonnaise, place the egg yolks, mustard and herbs in a bowl. Whisk well and quickly, then, continuing to whisk, add the oil, little by little, until you have a creamy mayonnaise. Add a few drops of vinegar or lemopn juice to thin the mixture to the preferred consistency.

When ready to serve the terrine, surround it with the rest of the jelly, chopped, accompanied by the herb mayonnaise and puréed vegetables.

---

touring around

Mons is magical, especially early in the morning. Perched on the crest of a hillside descending from the Provençal Alps, it's one of the most northerly points in the Var where the coast comes into view, albeit hazily far away. The village itself is a beautiful and strange grid of narrow streets overhung with arches. The language of its inhabitants still conserves some Ligurian Italian words. The people of Mons were totally wiped out in the Black Death of 1348; colonists from the area around Genoa and Ventimiglia were brought in to replace them.

Fayence, a village that has sprawled but still has moderate cuteness, has plenty of English inhabitants and estate agents. Built on a steep hillside, its road winds back and forth up to the centre, which is pleasant enough. There's a *mairie* perched on an arch over the main street, a forgotten 18th-century church and a view not to be missed from the Tour de l'Horloge at the very top of the village. Check what you can see against the ceramic panorama painted and baked into tiles under your hands. Potters, painters and antiques dealers have settled here, while gliders set off from close by.

Around lunch, tour old **Seillans** on foot. Enter via the 12th-century Porte Sarrasine opposite the hotel and framed by the *deux rocs*. Francine explained to us that these two rocks only reemerged from beneath the village in the 1960s when some medieval houses built over them collapsed! The Surrealist Max Ernst once had a house in the old centre, but the village looks like an archetypal old Provençal cliché. Seillans is one of the most beautiful villages in the country, according to its membership of the *association des plus beaux villages de France*. It has been occupied since the time of the Ligurians, giving it some two and a half millennia to perfect its charm. It has cobbled streets leading up to the castle (private property), once owned by Shirley Conran apparently. A couple of surprising modern statues are to be spotted in the streets, while a handful of galleries and exhibitions bring artistic life to the village in summer. Walk down to the Place Thouron. A splendid display of fresh flowers in pots was being watered in the splashing bowls of the fountain the day we were last there. *Boules* players take over the Place de la République above in the afternoon.

To sample the powerful, even overpowering products that flowers can produce, head for **Grasse**. It was Catherine de' Medici who introduced artichokes to the French and the scent trade to Grasse. Although it may seem obvious that a town set in the midst of France's natural floral hothouse should be a Mecca for perfume-making, Grasse's most important industry throughout the Middle Ages was tanning imported sheep-skins from the mountains of Provence and buffalo-hides from her Italian allies, Genoa and Tuscany. Part of the tanning process made use of the aromatic herbs that grew nearby, especially powdered myrtle which gave the leather a greenish lustre.

In Renaissance Italy, one of the most important status symbols an aristocrat could flaunt was fine, perfumed gloves. When Catherine asked Grasse, Tuscany's old trading partner, to start supplying them, the Grassois left the buffalo hides behind to become *gantiers parfumeurs*. When gloves fell out of fashion after the Revolution they became simply *parfumeurs*, and when Paris co-opted the business in the 1800s, the townspeople concentrated on what has been their speciality ever since—distilling the essences that go into that final costly tiny bottles.

The Cannes road leads into Grasse's promenade, Place du Cours, with pretty views over the countryside. Close by at 23 Bd. Fragonard is the Musée Villa Fragonard, ✆ 04 93 40 32 64 (*open summer 10am–7pm, winter 10am–12pm and 2–5pm, closed Mon, Tues, and Nov*), in a 17th-century home belonging to a cousin of Grasse's most famous citizen, Jean-Honoré Fragonard (1732–1806). Son of a *gantier parfumeur*, Fragonard expressed the inherent family sweetness in chocolate-box pastel portraits and mildly erotic rococo scenes of French royals trying their best to look like well-groomed poodles.

It's hard to miss the *parfumeries* in Grasse, and if you've read Patrick Süskind's novel *Perfume* the free tours may seem a bit bland. The alchemical processes of extracting essences from freshly cut mimosa, jasmine, roses, bitter orange and so on, are explained—you learn that it takes 900,000 rosebuds to make a kilo of rose essence, which then goes to the *haute couture* perfume-bottlers and hype-merchants of Paris. Even more alarming are some of the other ingredients that arouse human hormones: the genital secretions of Ethiopian cats, whale vomit, and Tibetan goat musk.

Tours in English are offered by Parfumerie Fragonard at 20 Bd. Fragonard; Les 4 Chemins, on the Route de Cannes; Molinard, 60 Bd. Victor-Hugo; and Gallimard, 73 Rte de Cannes (N85). The visits are free, and they don't seem to mind too much if you don't buy something at the end.

Between Grasse and Cannes, **Mougins** is one of the great destinations for modern-day culinary pilgrims in France. Roger Vergé's Le Moulin de Mougins, in a converted olive mill near Notre-Dame-de-Vie, is one of the most famous restaurants in the world. Roger Vergé is also author of the celebrated Provençal cookery book, *The Cuisine of the Sun*.

A Culinary Glossary

The full French culinary vocabulary is enormous, and several pocket guides are available that give extensive lists of the many terms and phrases. The following should, though, provide some of the necessary basics.

Useful Phrases

I'd like to book a table (for two/at 12.30pm)	*Je voudrais réserver une table (pour deux personnes/à midi et demie)*
lunch/dinner	*le déjeuner/le dîner*
Is it necessary to book for lunch/dinner today?	*Est-ce qu'il faut réserver pour déjeuner/dîner aujourd'hui?*
Waiter/Waitress! (to attract their attention)	*Monsieur/Madame/Mademoiselle! S'il vous plaît*
The 130F menu, please	*Le menu à cent trente francs, s'il vous plaît*
Which are your specialities?	*Quelles sont les specialités de la maison?*
What is (this dish), exactly?	*Qu'est-ce que c'est exactement, (ce plat)?*
The wine list, please	*La carte des vins, s'il vous plaît*
Another bottle of wine, please	*Une autre bouteille, s'il vous plaît*
water (from the tap, perfectly good in France, and usually given as a matter of course)	*une carafe d'eau*
mineral water/fizzy/still	*eau minérale/gazeuse/plate*
coffee (espresso)	*café*
white coffee	*café au lait /café crème*
That was wonderful	*C'était formidable/délicieux*
We've enjoyed the meal very much, thank you	*Nous avons très bien mangé, merci*
The bill, please	*L'addition, s'il vous plaît*

Poissons et Coquillages (Crustacés)
Fish and Shellfish

Aiglefin	Little haddock	*Cuisses de grenouilles*	Frogs' legs
Anchois	Anchovies	*Darne*	Thin slice of fish
Anguille	Eel	*Daurade*	Sea bream
Bar	Bass	*Ecrevisse*	Freshwater crayfish
Barbue	Brill		
Baudroie	Anglerfish	*Encornet*	Squid
Bigorneau	Winkle	*Eperlan*	Smelt
Blanchailles	Whitebait	*Escabèche*	Fish fried, marinated, and served cold
Bouillabaisse	Marseille's complex soup of mixed fish, served with *rouille*		
		Escargot	Snail
		Espadon	Swordfish
Bourride	Provençal soup of mixed fish, served with *aïoli*	*Flétan*	Halibut
		Friture	Deep fried fish
		Fruits de mer	Seafood
Brandade de morue	Salt cod with olive oil, garlic and cream added	*Gambas*	Giant prawn
		Gigot de mer	A large fish cooked whole
Brème	Bream		
Brochet	Pike	*Grondin*	Red gurnard
Bulot	Whelk	*Hareng*	Herring
Cabillaud	Fresh cod	*Homard*	Lobster
Calmar	Squid	*Huître*	Oyster
Carrelet	Plaice	*Julienne*	Ling
Colin	Hake	*Langouste*	Spiny Mediterranean lobster
Congre	Conger eel		
Coques	Cockles	*Langoustine*	Dublin Bay prawn
Coquilles St-Jacques	Scallops		
		Lieu	Pollack, coley
Crabe	Crab	*Limande*	Lemon sole
Crevette grise	Shrimp	*Lotte*	Monkfish
Crevette rose	Prawn	*Loup (de mer)*	Sea bass
		Maquereau	Mackerel

Merlan	Whiting	Rouget	Red mullet
Morue	Salt Cod	Saumon	Salmon
Moules	Mussels	Saint-Pierre	John Dory
Oursin	Sea urchin	Sole	Sole
Pageot	Sea bream	(à la meunière)	(with butter, lemon and parsley)
Palourde	Clam		
Pétoncle	Small scallop	Telline	Tiny clam
Poulpe	Octopus	Thon	Tuna
Poutargue	Grey mullet roe	Truite	Trout
Praire	Small clam	Truite saumonée	Salmon trout
Raie	Skate		
Rascasse	Scorpion fish	Vive	Weever

Viandes, Volaille, Charcuterie
(Meat, Poultry, Charcuterie)

Agneau (de pré salé)	Lamb (grazed in fields by the sea)	Carré	The best end of a cutlet or chop
Aile	Wing	Cervelles	Brains
Andouillette	Chitterling (tripe) sausage	Châteaubriand	Thick steak cut from the fillet of beef
Biftek	Beefsteak		
Blanc	Breast or white meat	Cheval	Horsemeat
		Chevreau	Kid
Blanquette	Stew of white meat, thickened with egg yolk	Civet	Stew, marinated in wine
Boeuf	Beef	Confit	Meat cooked and preserved in its own fat
Boudin blanc	Sausage of white meat		
Boudin noir	Black pudding	Contre-filet	Sirloin steak
Brochette	Meat (or fish) on a skewer	Côte, côtelette	Chop, cutlet
		Cuisse	Thigh or leg
Caille	Quail	Daube	Provençal stew with wine
Canard, caneton	Duck, duckling		
		Dinde, dindon	Turkey
		Eminced	Thin slice

Entrecôte	Ribsteak	*Oie*	Goose
Epaule	Shoulder	*Os*	Bone
Estouffade	A meat stew marinated, fried, and then braised	*Perdreau (perdrix)*	Partridge
		Petit salé	Salt pork
Faisan	Pheasant	*Pieds*	Trotters
Faux filet	Sirloin	*Pieds et paquets*	Tripe stuffed with garlic, onions and salt pork, traditionally (although rarely) served with calf's trotters
Foie	Liver		
Foie Gras	Fattened goose or duck liver		
Frais de veau	Veal testicles		
Fricadelle	Meatball		
Génisse	Heifer		
Gésier	Gizzard	*Pintade*	Guinea fowl
Gibier	Game	*Porc*	Pork
Gigot	Leg of lamb	*Poularde*	Capon
Gigue	Haunch	*Poulet*	Chicken
Graisse	Fat	*Poussin*	Baby chicken
Grillade	Grilled meat	*Queue de boeuf*	Oxtail
Grive	Thrush	*Ris (de veau)*	Sweetbreads (veal)
Jambon	Ham		
Jarret	Knuckle	*Rognon*	Kidney
Langue	Tongue	*Rôti*	Roast
Lapereau	Young rabbit	*Sanglier*	Wild boar
Lapin	Rabbit	*Saucisse*	Sausage
Lard (lardon)	Bacon (diced bacon)	*Saucisson*	Dry sausage, like salami
Lièvre	Hare	*Selle (d'agneau)*	Saddle (of lamb)
Magret (de canard)	Breast (of duck)		
Marcassin	Young wild boar	*Steak tartare*	Raw minced beef, often topped with a raw egg yolk
Merguez	Spicy red sausage		
Museau	Muzzle		
Navarin	Lamb stew with root vegetables	*Suprême de volaille*	Fillet of chicken breast and wing
Noix de veau	Topside of veal	*Tête (de veau)*	Head (calf's)

Taureau	Bull's meat	*Travers de porc*	Spare ribs
Tortue	Turtle	*Tripes*	Tripe
Tournedos	Thick round slices of beef fillet	*Veau*	Veal
		Venaison	Venison

Cooking Terms for Steaks and Grills

bleu	very rare	*à point*	medium rare
saignant	rare	*bien cuit*	well done

Légumes, Herbes, Épices
(Vegetables, Herbs, Spices)

Aïgo boulido	Garlic soup	*Céleri (-rave)*	Celery (celeriac)
Ail	Garlic	*Cèpe*	Cep (wild dark brown mushroom)
Aïoli (le grand)	Provençal garlic mayonnaise (with salt cod, mixed vegetables and possibly snails)	*Champignon*	Mushroom
		Chanterelle	Wild yellow mushroom
		Chicorée	Curly endive
Algue	Seaweed	*Chou*	Cabbage
Aneth	Dill	*Choufleur*	Cauliflower
Artichaut (à la barigoule)	Artichoke (with wine and olive oil, maybe stuffed with mushrooms)	*Choucroute*	Pickled white cabbage
		Ciboulette	Chives
		Citrouille	Pumpkin
Asperge	Asparagus	*Coeur de palmier*	Heart of palm
Aubergine	Aubergine (eggplant)	*Concombre*	Cucumber
Avocat	Avocado	*Cornichon*	Gherkin
Basilic	Basil	*Courgette*	Courgette (zucchini)
Betterave	Beetroot		
Blette	Swiss chard	*Cresson*	Watercress
Cannelle	Cinnamon	*Echalote*	Shallot
Cébette	New onion	*Endive*	Chicory

Epeautre	Einkorn or German wheat	*Persil*	Parsley
Epinards	Spinach	*Piment*	Pimento
Estragon	Tarragon	*Pissenlits*	Dandelion greens
Fenouil	Fennel	*Pistou*	Basil, garlic and parmesan mixed together
Fève	Broad bean		
Fleur de courgette	Courgette flower	*Poireau*	Leek
Frites	Chips (French fries)	*Pois chiche*	Chickpea
		Pois	Pea
Genièvre	Juniper	*Poivron*	Bell pepper
Gingembre	Ginger	*Pomme d'amour*	Tomato
Girofle	Clove	*Pomme de terre*	Potato
Gousse d'ail	Clove of garlic	*Potiron*	Pumpkin
Haricot (rouge, blanc)	Bean (kidney, white)	*Primeurs*	Young vegetables
Haricot vert	Green (French) bean	*Radis*	Radish
		Raifort	Horseradish
Jardinière	With diced garden vegetables	*Ratatouille*	Mixed vegetables (aubergines, courgettes, tomatoes, peppers, onions, cooked with olive oil and garlic)
Laitue	Lettuce		
Laurier	Bay leaf		
Lentille	Lentil		
Maïs (épis de)	Sweet corn (on the cob)		
		Riz	Rice
Marjolaine	Marjoram	*Romarin*	Rosemary
Menthe	Mint	*Safran*	Saffron
Mesclun	Salad of various leaves	*Salade verte*	Green salad
		Salé	Salted
Morille	Morel mushroom	*Sarrasin*	Buckwheat
		Sarriette	Savory (the herb)
Moutarde	Mustard		
Navet	Turnip		
Oignon	Onion	*Sauge*	Sage
Oseille	Sorrel	*Seigle*	Rye
Panais	Parsnip	*Serpolet*	Wild thyme

			prepared with rice and egg in a brown earthenware dish
Tapenade	Paste of olives, capers and garlic (sometimes with anchovies)		
Thym	Thyme	*Truffe*	Truffle
Tian	Vegetable normally	*Verveine*	Verbena

Fruits, Noix, Desserts (Fruits, Nuts, Desserts)

Abricot	Apricot	*Clafoutis*	Fruit flan
Amande	Almond	*Coing*	Quince
Ananas	Pineapple	*Compote*	Stewed fruit
Banane	Banana	*Corbeille de fruits*	Basket of fruit
Bavarois	Mousse or custard in mould	*Coupe*	Dish of ice cream
Bombe	Ice-cream dessert in round mould	*Crème anglaise*	Thin custard
		Crème Chantilly	Sweet whipped cream
Bonbon	Sweet, candy		
Brebis, fromage de	Ewe's milk cheese	*Crème pâtissière*	Thick custard
		Datte	Date
Brioche	Light sweet yeast bread	*Faisselle*	Strained fromage frais
Brugnon	Nectarine	*Figue*	Fig
Cacahouète	Peanut	*(de Barbarie)*	(prickly pear)
Cassis	Blackcurrant	*Flan*	Custard baked in a mould (not a flan)
Cerise	Cherry		
Charlotte	Baked dessert, with layers of fruit in a sponge finger, cake or bread surround, served hot or cold	*Fraise*	Strawberry
		(des bois)	(wild)
		Framboise	Raspberry
		Fromage	Cheese
		(plateau de)	(board)
Chausson	Turnover	*Fruits confits*	Candied or *glacé* fruits
Chèvre, fromage de	Goat's milk cheese	*Fruit de la passion*	Passion fruit
Citron	Lemon		
Citron vert	Lime	*Gâteau*	Cake

Génoise	Rich sponge cake	*Sablé*	Shortbread
Glace	Ice cream	*Savarin*	A filled cake, shaped like a ring
Grenade	Pomegranate		
Groseille	Redcurrant, gooseberry		
		Tarte, tartelette	Tart, little tart
Lavande	Lavender	*Tarte Tropézienne*	Sponge cake filled with custard and topped with nuts
Madeleine	Small sponge cake		
Mandarine	Tangerine	*Truffe*	Chocolate truffle
Mangue	Mango	*Noisette*	Hazelnut
Marron	Chestnut	*Noix (de cajou)*	Nut or walnut
Merise	Wild cherry	*Pamplemousse*	Grapefruit
Miel	Honey	*Parfait*	Frozen mousse
Mirabelle	Mirabelle plum (small, round and orangey-yellow)	*Pastèque*	Water melon
		Pêche (blanche)	Peach (white)
		Petits fours	Tiny cakes and pastries
Mûre	Blackberry, mulberry	*Pignon*	Pine nut
		Pistache	Pistachio
Myrtille	Bilberry	*Poire*	Pear
Noisette	Hazelnut	*Pomme*	Apple
Noix (de cajou)	Nut or walnut (cashew nut)	*Prune*	Plum
		Pruneau	Prune
Pamplemousse	Grapefruit	*Raisin (sec)*	Grape (raisin)
Parfait	Frozen mousse	*Reine-Claude*	Greengage
Pastèque	Water melon	*Sablé*	Shortbread
Pêche (blanche)	Peach (white)	*Savarin*	A filled cake, shaped like a ring
Petits fours	Tiny pastries		
Pignon	Pine nut		
Pistache	Pistachio	*Tarte, tartelette*	Tart, little tart
Poire	Pear	*Tarte Tropézienne*	Sponge cake filled with custard and topped with nuts
Pomme	Apple		
Prune	Plum		
Pruneau	Prune		
Raisin (sec)	Grape (raisin)	*Truffe*	Chocolate truffle
Reine-Claude	Greengage		

Cooking Terms, Miscellaneous, Snacks

Aigre-doux	Sweet and sour	*Chaud*	Hot
Aiguillette	Thin slice	*Chou*	Puff pastry
A *l'anglaise*	Boiled	*Confiture*	Jam
A *l'arlésienne*	With aubergines, potatoes, tomatoes, onions, rice	*Couteau*	Knife
		Crème	Cream
		Crêpe	Thin pancake
A *la grecque*	Cooked in olive oil and lemon	*Croque-monsieur*	Toasted ham and cheese sandwich
A *la provençale*	Cooked with tomatoes, garlic, olive oil	*Croustade*	Small savoury pastry
Allumette	Strip of puff pastry	*Cru*	Raw
		Cuillère	Spoon
Amuse-gueule	Appetizer	*Cuit (au feu de bois)*	Cooked (over a wood fire)
Assiette de...	Plate or platter of...		
		Diable	Spicy mustard sauce
Barquette	Pastry boat		
Béarnaise	Sauce of egg yolks, shallots, tarragon and white wine	*Emincé*	Thinly sliced
		En croûte	Cooked in a pastry crust
		En papillote	Baked in buttered paper
Béchamel	White sauce of butter, flour and milk		
		Epices	Spices
		Farci	Stuffed
Beignet	Fritter	*Feuilleté*	Flaky pastry
Beurre	Butter	*Flambé*	Set aflame with alcohol
Beurre blanc	Reduced sauce of butter, white wine, vinegar, shallots		
		Forestière	With bacon and mushrooms
		Fourchette	Fork
Bordelaise	Red wine, bone marrow and shallot sauce	*Four*	Oven
		Fourré	Stuffed
		Frais, fraîche	Fresh
Chasseur	Mushrooms and shallots in white wine	*Frappé*	With crushed ice
		Frit	Fried

Froid	Cold	Piquante	Vinegar sauce with shallots and capers
Fromage (de brebis, de chèvre)	Cheese (ewe's, goat's)	Pissaladière	A kind of Provençal pizza with onions, anchovies, etc.
Fumé	Smoked		
Galantine	Cooked, pressed meat served in cold jelly		
		Poché	Poached
Galette	Pancake	Poivre	Pepper
Garni	With vegetables	Quenelles	Dumplings
(au) Gratin	Topped with crisp browned cheese and breadcrumbs	Raclette	Toasted cheese with potatoes, onions and pickles
Grillé	Grilled		
Hachis	Mince or minced	Rouille	Thick sauce of egg yolks, garlic, saffron, chili or cayenne pepper and fish stock
Hollandaise	A sauce of butter and vinegar		
Huile (d'olive)	Oil (olive)		
Marmite	Casserole		
Médaillon	Round piece	Salé	Salted, spicy
Mijoté	Simmered	Sanglant	Rare steak
Mornay	Cheese sauce	Sel	Salt
Nouilles	Noodles	Sucre	Sugar
Oeuf (brouillé)	Egg (scrambled)	Sucré	Sweet
		Tilleul	Lime (-blossom)
Pain	Bread	Timbale	Pie cooked in a dome-shaped mould
Pan Bagna	Slices of peppers and egg served with olive oil, lemon juice and garlic on bread		
		Tranche	Slice
		Vapeur	Steamed
Pané	Breaded	Véronique	Green grapes, wine, and cream sauce
Parmentier	With potatoes		
Pâte	Pastry, pasta		
Paupiette	Rolled and filled thin slices of fish or meat	Vinaigre	Vinegar
		Vinaigrette	Oil and vinegar dressing
Pavé	Slab		